More Village Idiot Reviews

PETE SORTWELL

Copyright © 2013 Pete Sortwell

All rights reserved.

ISBN: 149098321X
ISBN-13: 978-1490983219

DEDICATION

To my mate James Vickery.

ACKNOWLEDGEMENTS

I wouldn't be able to get my work into your hands if it wasn't for the help of the team I employ, they work extremely hard to make sure what ends up on your kindle is a high quality. These people are:

Julie Lewthwaite, for her continued sterling work on turning my ramblings into something that I can charge money for.
http://www.mlwritingservices.co.uk/

Graham D. Lock, for the excellent covers he's provided me. http://www.peopleperhour.com/people/graham-d/animator-graphic-designer-and-illu/177926

I can't recommend these people enough.

DISCLAIMER

More Village Idiot Reviews is a comedy by Pete Sortwell and is not intended maliciously. Pete Sortwell has invented all names and situations in the stories, except in cases when public figures are being satirised. Any other use of real names is accidental and coincidental.

INTRODUCTION

Well, it's been almost eight months since the release of the first book, *The Village Idiot Reviews*. It's been a fantastic success, if I do say so myself. Who knew that a book I wrote to cheer myself up would be enjoyed by so many people? If you're returning because of reading and enjoying the first book, thank you so much for downloading it and taking a chance on a new author with a new kind of book. If you're a new reader to this series, then fear not: this book is also written to be enjoyed as a standalone. You can read the first one later as a prequel.

All your favourite characters are back; I've also created a couple of new ones. So sit back, relax and get ready for *More Village Idiot Reviews*.

TCP ORIGINAL ANTISEPTIC LIQUID 200ML

Just don't put on the sore patch that used to be your nipples.

I'll start by saying: I bought the Spanish version of this. But it was still called TCP, how amazing is that!? I did fear that they'd have called it something else and I'm so glad they hadn't.

I found myself in need of this while on my honeymoon. Which wasn't something I'd planned for, but then I don't suppose anyone ever planned the need for TCP, unless they were drastically weird or something — which I'm not.

As is the norm in Spain, I hired a little moped. Mary, my new wife, refused to come with me on a trip to the local monastery. The moped I hired wasn't in the best condition but, as Pedro informed me, the leopard-skin seat made up for any mechanical shortcomings. He was right, too; everyone was looking at me as I chugged my way through the local town. Mind you, I think the young ladies might have been looking at me just as much as they were looking at the sex-mobile that I was riding.

Seeing as I was on holiday I wore the uniform all vicars wear when out of sight of their flock — Speedos. The smaller the better, we all wear them on holiday; well, after a long year of wearing our robes and tight-necked dog collars, a small pant-like trunk is extremely liberating. I could feel the wind on the inside of my thighs, airing Jesus and the two disciples, Peter and Nathanael. I bloody loved it. The only thing that would have made it better was my old large hip flask, but seeing as Mary had pronounced me an alcoholic, I wasn't allowed it on the holiday.

The monastery was at the top of a mountain so I was soon out on the open road. Getting up the hill took a little longer than if I'd been walking, but it was steep so I was happy that I didn't have to actually walk, and I managed to ignore the kids that strolled past me as I was crawling up the hill on Pedro's trusty moped. They were just jealous that I was burning my bare feet on metal and not on the road like they were.

Meeting the Spanish vicars was nice. I couldn't understand a word they were saying, but we pointed at the Bible and nodded in agreement a fair amount. After tea it was time to head back down the hill. Unfortunately, this was when I found the brakes weren't all they should have been and I got the speed wobbles. Luckily I was only on the first corner so wasn't going as fast as I imagine I would have been if I'd careered all the way down. I still hit the ground at some pace, though, and it seemed for a while that the pace would continue. That part of the road had recently been tarmacked, so was fairly smooth for me to skid on. I didn't feel the pain until I'd stopped and the heat from the road brought me out of the daze I was in. My Speedos had disintegrated somewhere along the way. I'd been on my front as I skidded and looking down, I noticed that the little Pope had lost some of his skin. It wasn't until later I realised that I'd lost most of my nipples, too. In the police car that took me home I caught a glimpse of my chest in the mirror. Next thing I know I'm waking up with the bed sheets my wife had lovingly placed over me stuck to me! The pain started all over again.

Mary had also forgotten to get holiday insurance, so with no choice but to take my healthcare into my own hands, I headed down to the chemist to see what I could lay my hands on for under five Euros. (I'd spent all my holiday money on the moped rental.)

I think the chemist must have been a sadist or something because the smile that appeared on his face when I showed him my scarred body was not something I expected. The smile grew as he handed me the bottle of TCP and waved his hand in dismissal when I offered him payment.

When you go on holiday, you don't expect to have to deal with the police once, let alone twice. I'd almost stopped screaming by the time they arrived at the villa. Apparently they were responding to reports of a little girl being murdered. In my defence, it wasn't like if you hurt yourself normally, this pain got worse as time went on, even if you weren't dabbing the area with a TCP-soaked bit of cotton wool.

Thankfully it was the second but last day of the holiday, so I didn't have long to wait before I could see a British doctor who didn't demand payment upfront before he let me take my T-shirt off. Unfortunately for me, scabs had started to form by then and he had to tear them off to get the bits of gravel out of my body that had lodged there during the accident. When I left the surgery I asked if there was anything I needed to do with the wounds while they healed. His answer? TCP. I didn't say anything, though, as us vicars aren't allowed to swear.

I kept the bottle of TCP and it's come in handy for the locals. Jock knocked our door late one night; something had bitten him, so I lent him a bit of this. I was glad to see that he screamed like a little girl, same as I did when I first applied it. Jock is an old biker chap so it means I'm not as soft as the people who were laughing at me thought I was.

-Father Frederick

BECOME A SCOTTISH LAIRD/LADY

Born into money but no title? This is for you.

Monty's the name, lording is the game. Which, to be honest, is a little troublesome if you don't have the title of 'Lord'. I'm rich, sure. But due to an upsetting incident in 1951, in which my father accidentally hit Winston Churchill in the corkers with a croquet mallet, he wasn't given the title he'd been promised. It was all wrong and if Churchill hadn't been so much of a bloody hero, the papers would have been all over the fact he took a large amount of money from my father to fund his last political campaign. All this meant that there was no title to come to me with the house and land in my inheritance. My father never got over the fact that he was to die like a normal man; we told everyone we were Lords. In fact the Sheptons have been telling people that for centuries, and until that fateful game of croquet, we were in line to be actual Lords. Father said he'd even been promised his own sword, too, so it was a double loss for him. Me? I've got my gamekeeper, Chopper, so I don't need a sword. Any trouble, I just point him at it and let him off his lead. Metaphorical lead, that is. You're not allowed to keep your own staff tied up in this day and age.

As I said, I've got it all; heirlooms from the ages, most touched or owned by people of substance. My gamekeeper, Chopper, is always getting his hands on things to add to the collection. I've a feeling he's a very good cat burglar and when we get back from a shoot somewhere he'll always produce something that I know not to ask questions about. I pay him well for it and add to the family collection of antiques and relics. This title really was the only thing that was missing from my life.

So once this wondrous thing called the Internet came out, I finally ended the age-old family tradition of getting ripped off by people who claimed they could sell us a title. I found this little beauty and can you believe the price! Under fifty new pounds — to be a Lord!

I purchased it in no time. Apparently all you do is purchase a square centimetre of land in Scotland and under law you're allowed to call yourself a Lord. Brilliant. I got straight on the phone and bought a square mile. It means I've bought all the other centimetres that people have bought from this company and that they can't now call themselves Lords, but then it shouldn't be the case that anyone with fifty pounds can do it. You should have years of wealth in your bloodline, land, cattle, a gamekeeper. So not only I am Lord of my own manor in the village where I live (I won't name it as there are more than a hundred ex Lords and Ladies that would quite like to know where I live at the moment), I'm also a living Lord in Scotland. I'm considering sending Chopper up there and seeing if he can pull a band of men together to build me a castle. Although I think castles are quite expensive these days and I don't want to have to sell any of the artwork, so it might be a project for a couple of years' time.

Being rich, I also opted for the cufflinks with the family coat of arms. We've had our coat of arms since Nelson drew them on a scrap of paper (before he lost his drawing arm) in whatever year it was Nelson lived. Just another little bit of background to my story and how, if you are one of the people who have lost your title, you should really feel grateful that someone from such good stock as me now holds it.

So if you're reading this and you are one of those people, all I can say is I'm sorry. I don't mean it, but I'm sure you understand that I'm better than you and deserve it more. Let's face it, you were probably punching well above your weight by calling yourself a Lord in the first place.

I will tell you, though, it feels great to be an actual Lord rather than a fat old fraud.

Tally ho!

-Monty

SAFARI AERO JAVELIN 600G

You need to choose this OR a stick. Never both.

I recently bought the Safari Aero javelin, it's something that I've been meaning to take up since school. I used to like a bit of shot-put too, but I had to stop that after I accidently messed my pants during the village version of the Highland Games. They're just too heavy and at my age, you just can't trust a fart enough to be throwing heavy things around from a squatting position — especially not when you're wearing a traditional Scottish kilt, with no underwear. It still hurts me to talk about. Ethel, the local crazy, was seen stuffing the kilt into her bag after I'd discarded it into the nearest garden.

So as you can see, my need for lighter things to throw was somewhat urgent. I read the product description with great interest; however, I'd like to let people know that if, like me, you go on YouTube for tips and you see a video that advises you to use a stick to practice with before you take up a javelin, please listen to my experience of it. I watched the video. The wait for the Safari Aero was fairly long, so I popped over the road to kick down some of Brian's trees to use for sticks. (It's OK because no one likes him, so even if they saw me doing it, they wouldn't have told him.) Then I went out in the park behind the Co-op to practise. I think I got the stance down to a tee within the first ten throws on the first day, then I was out every day, as much as I could. I even felt my aim and strength improving. I'd sprayed a target onto the hedge and it caught the sticks; it was a fairly robust thicket.

You can imagine my enthusiasm for the actual javelin pole to arrive, and after the allotted three weeks, it did. I'd got a matching vest for the big day and slipped the singlet on in double-quick time and headed out to the park. This is where my gripe comes in: the javelin is actually a lot lighter and more aero-dynamic than a stick, so when I threw it, it went sailing over the hedge and beyond, into the Co-op car park. By the time I got round there, it had gone. No doubt Ethel had seen it and taken it home to train runner beans up. I'd go round and challenge her, but she's been known to carry a police baton, and to bite.

Personally I feel hurt by the whole situation and have decided to go back to throwing sticks, although I'll have to find a new garden to get them from as I've taken all the branches from Brian's trees.

So, my advice to you if you're thinking of buying one of these bad boys, is wait for it to come, don't bother with the sticks, or just throw sticks instead. Whatever you start with, stay with.

-Jock

30 METRE COIL 30M 100FT RETRACTABLE GARDEN HOSE REEL PIPE WITH SPRAY GUN NOZZLE

Good for keeping control of your boss.

I'm a gamekeeper by trade, always have been. However, my boss is a bit of a penis and thinks I'm more along the line of a slave, or dogsbody. He has me doing all sorts; cutting the grass, clearing the guttering, it's never ending. If there were more gamekeeping jobs in the area, then I'd leave. However 'Lord' Monty owns all the land around here, and I don't like travelling further than I can see.

Last week, he decided that rather than prance about the grounds in the tight trousers that he thinks make him look like a horse rider, but actually make everyone else think he's bent, that he'd go and try and find a poacher who's been causing trouble in the woods. Now, this is my job and if you saw Monty you'd know that he isn't the sort of person that would know what to do if he was to come face to face with some of the rough sorts that think stealing wild birds is a valid career choice. He's fat. No, actually he's morbidly obese, according to his doctor. He looks like a whale in leggings, all spilling over the sides. A truly horrible man.

So it's the little things that I can do to make his day a little worse that keep me going.

As I said, last week he wobbled off into the woods to scare the people who were stealing his birds. It didn't work and he ended up in a pile of stinging nettles screaming like a small child that had just looked round to find his parents weren't following him after all. Crying and sniffling, he was, all the way home, where he found me. Turns out someone had taken offence to the fat oaf hiding in the bushes and looking at her, and had given him a quick blast with the pepper spray she had in her bag. I'd guess a fox had urinated all over him, too, as he definitely stated that he didn't wet himself, but there was a wet patch on his trousers. Still, if he says a fox did it, then we'll go with that. Either way, I got to give him a rough time of it.

I told him that it takes half an hour of blasting water in the eyes to stop the burning. I've no idea if it's true or not, but he let me hold this hose over his face, nose and mouth for the full half an hour. It was brilliant, seeing him flounder about on the ground. It reminded me of seeing the people on the news trying to keep a beached whale alive. If I'd had a sponge handy I'd have dropped that on his face a couple of times too, it could have been like waterboarding a fat terrorist. I didn't, though, so I just had to hold the handle so tight on the fastest blast it would do. So hard in fact, that I broke it. That's why I've bought another one. The process was easy, delivery came the next day, and now it's all hanging up ready in the shed for the next time Monty wants to do my bloody job for me.

-Chopper

LG 50PA4500 50-INCH HD READY PLASMA TV WITH FREEVIEW AND 2 HDMI PORTS

So big it's like the TV stars are in the room.

I recently popped into a high street store to purchase a new TV set for me and my new bride, Janet; after a long and relaxing honeymoon in the Gulf of Skegness, we decided we'd like to spend the remaining summer evenings at home watching DVD box sets of *Cheers*, and to do so on a larger TV than we've ever had before was the plan.

    When we popped into the shop at Southampton Park Farm Retail Estate, we were greeted by a store full of people who can only be described as dirty. I'm not sure if there had been a water shortage and washing had been a problem in the area that week, as our village had been fine. Mind you, we did travel for half an hour by bus, so it might have been a more local problem, but as sure as I'm a *Cheers* fan, these people stank. They smelled so bad I had to open the fire exit door to get some air. Unfortunately I was sick as soon as the air hit me. I would have told the staff at the store, but didn't in case they made me clean it up.

    When questioned, the staff in the store explained that they had no control over who came in and who didn't, but I've checked consumer law on this, and also the trespassing one, and I've found out that if you're in business you're allowed to sell to whoever you want to and if you do not want someone in your store, for whatever reason, then you have every right to ask them to leave. Maybe this is something that the staff should have done last Saturday.

For this reason (and the fact that my wife refused to do a two-man lift on a large TV all the way home) I decided to buy online. The TV that came was just as described and I didn't even need to carry it into the house. The courier did it for me.

We've now been enjoying the *Cheers* gang for a couple of weeks. Sam is almost life-sized in my living room. I've always wanted to meet him and this TV has almost made that possible. Although it would be better to actually meet him. When he finally decides to reply to one of my letters I might get the opportunity.

-Brian

HUNTER OUTDOOR HORSEMAN UNISEX WAX JACKET

A little bit too country.

Being a Lord and a land owner, it is imperative that I look the part. My land spans almost twenty miles, squared. Most days I get my gamekeeper, Chopper, to keep his eyes on things; however, sometimes I like to get out there and make sure everything is running as it should be. This jacket helps me blend in, and recently I needed to do some serious blending.

I needed to get an extra large one as, being rich, it's hard to constrain your diet to rabbit food. I love meat, cheese and fat. And living in the country and owning livestock, I have all the meat, cheese and fat you can shake a fat Lord at.

We've had a couple of problems on one of the farms during the last year or so with a sheep being killed and then someone touching up one of the cows. Recently we've had someone running through the West Woods screaming sexual obscenities. Bert, the farmer who owned said sheep, was convinced that it's the local vicar, Father Frederick. I wasn't so sure as I know Fred and he's always been a pretty decent chap, not a pervert or anything. If it was anyone, I'd say it was that gypsy fellow who turned up about a year ago. You can't trust a man that is happy living in something smaller than one of my downstairs toilets.

All day I was waiting in the woods, standing in the undergrowth. I should have listened to Chopper; this jacket was a little too well-camouflaged. As I was hiding not too far away from the path (I wanted to be able to grab the dirty swine if he showed his face) a young woman walked past. I didn't say anything, but the dog she was with started barking and pulling her towards me; this caused her to look into the trees and that was when she saw my face peering out at her. The scream almost deafened me. The dog kept on barking and what with that and the woman screaming, I got disorientated and tried to walk towards her, if only to calm her down and let her know she wasn't in any danger. It was then I felt the stinging burn in my eyes, nose and throat. She'd gassed me and I was going down, right into the patch of stinging nettles I'd been standing next to.

I don't know how long I was down for, long enough for the woman to have completely disappeared by the time I emerged. I managed to get home and Chopper had to hose me down for thirty minutes to get the pepper spray out of my eyes.

I almost choked on the water, but Chopper assured me that it takes the full half hour for the burning to stop. The nettle stings took a while longer, but for most of the time I was more concerned about the other pain in my face, so it wasn't too bad. I got the white lumps that come out after a sting and for the rest of the day I looked like I'd got a dose of something nasty.

This jacket is good. It stopped me from getting too wet during the soaking. It was also very good at only allowing my exposed flesh to get stung by the nettles, which meant face and hands. If you need a good quality country jacket for walking in — or indeed around — undergrowth, then this is the purchase you should be making.

-Monty

CABIN MAX GLOBAL — EXTRA LARGE 107L LIGHTWEIGHT FOLDING TROLLEY SUITCASE LUGGAGE 71 X 46 X 33CM

Get smaller ones.

I left the care home I've lived at for years last week and needed a big bag to cart all my stuff away. The council got me a flat in the village I used to live in so I was happy. Moving day went well and the bag held all it needed to, with me needing just a small carrier to put my delicates in; my glass bong and such like.

I would offer a word of warning about this bag, though. If you buy it, don't leave it outside your door while you carry the microwave you've nicked from the care home/your parents' house into your flat or, like me, you could lose all of your clothes. If I'd thought about it I would have bought three smaller bags, then there'd have been no way someone could wheel them all away. I didn't, though, I went for quickness and suffered the consequences.

I've never had to deal with the police from the complainant's point of view; I thought they'd be less patronising. They weren't, though, they seemed almost happy that it had happened to me for once.

I thought I was the only thief around here. Still, Social Services have a duty to buy me all new stuff so it's not too bad. I am, however, going to make it my mission to find out who nicked it so I can keep the money for the new kit.

-Denny

ECHO MIKE

Better than the real thing.

I love singing, always have. In fact I love music, full stop. From when I wake up in the morning to when I put the chickens to bed at night, all I think about is music. Well, that and all the other things I think about, but I do have my inside radio on almost always. I try not to have it on whilst on the toilet as it's not the British way. No, I have the bathroom radio on then, just so no one can hear me during my gentleman's sit down. It wouldn't be British to do anything else. Unless there isn't a radio in the bathroom, then I just turn the tap on full and hope it doesn't splash out the basin and wet my trousers while they're on the floor.

I've digressed, though. As I was saying, I love music. I sing it while Janet, my wife, is out. Sometimes I even walk across the field and sing while I'm walking. I enjoy it immensely and there isn't anyone around to tell me I can't sing or to shut up.

I'd like nothing better but to go to the monthly karaoke night held at the Lamb and Whistle. I can't, though as Jock ruins my evening every time I try and do something musical. Jock is a bully who doesn't like anyone but him being musical. He thinks he is dead hard because he used to be in a biker band. He's not, though, he's just old and still wears his thinning grey hair in a ponytail, along with his 1973 leather jacket and trousers. It all stems from the first time I met him and mistook him for a *Grease* fan. I seriously thought he was in full T-bird regalia. How was I supposed to know people still dressed like that these days?

Anyway, regardless of how silly he looks, I won't be attending the pub for anything anymore. He dragged me outside not so long ago and all I did was try and audition for his band. I actually think he was quite small-minded to think that a metal band *doesn't* need a good maracas player. He does, though, and that's why he did what he did.

I think most people would use the Xbox and one of the SingStar programs to sing at home; those people don't know the words to the songs, though. I can confidently say that I know every song by Barry White off by heart. I've also got my inside radio to play the music, so this microphone is great for me to use either in the house or in the fields. It doesn't need electricity either. It just brings a professional feel to the singing and the echo is something that I doubt an Xbox game could do anyway.

It's a great mic, I suppose kids could use it too. The colour is great and I've not lost it yet. It's also pretty much unbreakable, I've dropped it over one hundred times and it's still working fine.

If you like singing and love Barry White, this is a great item to spend your money on. It makes me feel so good to hold it in my hand. I've got a huge white suit that I wear, too. I bought it off eBay and the seller promised me it used to belong to Barry himself, although I didn't think Barry was as thin as this suit seems to suggest. Still, I don't like to think the worst of people so if the seller says it was Barry's, that's what I'm going to tell people. I've not blacked up or had my hair put into dreads yet. I don't think it's very PC to dress up like your heroes if it means using boot polish. I can't run the risk of being called a racist. Being called an idiot is bad enough. I don't want the *Daily Mail* turning up to give me a medal and making me join their racist club or anything. No, the suit and pink silk shirt is more than enough. If anyone is in any doubt as to who I'm dressed up as, I'll make a Barry White name badge.

One thing I noticed about Barry is that he never really did much dancing. I dance. I have to. So I incorporate a bit of

John Travolta from *Saturday Night Fever* when I sing. It's a real shame I can't go and put the show on in the pub for the locals. Maybe if I pray really hard one day God will make Jock stop being nasty and allow me in. Until then I'll stick with the living room and the fields.

I will say, though, if you do buy this, don't take it into work and use it in the toilets. People complain to the boss when you do that. Use your inside voice for work singing. In fact, as a general rule, try not to have any sit downs while you're at work; the taps are too far away and they don't generally have radios in. People just come in and turn the taps off, normally just in time to hear the mother of all plonks.

Maybe that's too much information, but I like to give a little background detail just in case someone thinking about buying this product is in the same position as me.

-Brian

SLX 27884K 48 ELEMENT DIGITAL TV AERIAL KIT

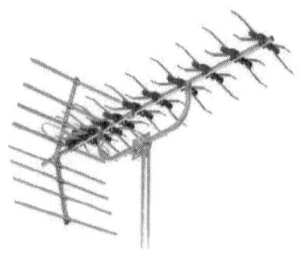

Just get a professional.

What with purchasing a new TV recently, I purchased this to make absolutely sure that I was getting the highest quality HD signal that I could. This seemed to be the aerial for the job. Not too expensive and no bus journey required to collect it.

Now, I'm not the most technical man in the world, but I know what I want and I'll do what I need to get it. I'm also a bit of a fiddler, unless we're talking bras, then I think fumbler would be a more accurate description. I had to borrow a ladder as the one I made out of pallets had to be taken down after Emma, the landlady from the pub, came and demanded to know why I'd destroyed the packaging that the brewery pick up the empty barrels in. It was almost dark by the time I'd finished putting them all back into their original form. Luckily I managed to convince my cousin, Jeff, to lend me his metal ladder and once I'd given him strict instructions to make sure he picked up next door's recycling bin that I knocked over putting the ladder up, then to stand with one foot on the bottom step, I went up ... then back down again as I forgot to take the aerial with me. The ladder didn't quite reach the guttering, but I felt confident that I could climb over, and I was right, I could. The aerial was simple to install: there was a pole on my chimney from the old analogue one so it was just a case of screwing the new one to it and feeding the wire down the chimney; we don't use the fireplace now, so I thought it would be better than drilling holes in the attic and the ceiling.

By the time I got to coming back down, Jeff had wandered off somewhere. But that was the least of my problems. I'd climbed over the guttering easily enough going up, but now I had to try and do the reverse. It wasn't an easy task and all it resulted in was me lying spread-eagled on the edge of the roof with my feet hanging over the gutters. I don't think I've ever been as scared in my life. All I could think to do was scream Jeff's name over and over again. It was fully dark by this time and it must have taken a good fifteen minutes before I heard Jeff laughing from the other side of the road. I wanted to shout out that it was no laughing matter, especially as my hands were sweating, but I couldn't though, all I could do was continue shouting his name, I couldn't even look round and see if he was still there. After a couple more terrifying minutes Jeff popped his head up next to my feet, grinning like the idiot he is. Then he asked why I hadn't gone up on the flat roof of the kitchen and climbed from there. That, it seems, was where he'd been. He then pushed my feet, allowing me to get some foothold in order to climb over the roof and come down the back way.

Once I'd had a cup of strong sweet tea to calm my nerves, we plugged the TV in and sat down to watch CBBC. Nothing. Not a sausage. So, getting my hat with the torch on, I headed back up to the roof. Jeff had gone to bed as soon as the biscuits ran out so I was on my own, although it wasn't that hard to get up there using the kitchen roof method. I saw the problem straight away; I'd forgotten to connect the lead to the actual aerial. An easy fix. The TV worked, although I wasn't happy with the picture, in fact I found myself up and down from the roof several times that night trying to make it perfect. It was about midnight when I headed up for the last time and I was being as delicate as possible with the aerial. The village was quiet, which it tends to be most of the time, but at night it is even more so. All of a sudden someone shouted, 'I'm not a man,' really loud. This caused me to jump. I slipped from the crouched position and started rolling down the wrong side of the roof. People say when you're dying, your life flashes in front of your eyes. That isn't true, I just thought, 'I'm slipping down a roof, I'll probably die. Yep, this is going to *really* hurt.' Nothing more, although it was saturated in complete fear. There was a scream too, just as I toppled over the guttering and headed face down towards the path below.

Thank God Jeff hadn't picked up the recycling bin like I'd told him, as I landed on that and squashed it almost flat. It was one of the most terrifying experiences of my life. If I was going to kill myself, I wouldn't do it by jumping off something. I think I'd want my last thoughts to be more along the lines of 'Sleep is coming' rather than a load of swear words.

So what I'd say about this aerial is, get someone who knows what they're doing to put it up for you. Not everyone will have as much dumb luck as I did. I'm going to get Jeff to apologise about the bin. Mrs Copperfield already hates me and she can't have heard what was happening or she'd have been out with the kettle to pour boiling water over me as I picked myself up. I still don't know who it was shouting in the street, but if I find out I've a good mind to tell them off.

-Brian

FARM CARE ELECTRIC FENCING EQUINE STARTER KIT

Buzzing.

As an award winning farmer, I've always prided myself on my ability to keep control of my livestock. Not once in my career have I needed to keep my animals under control with a stun gun or electric fence. However, I found myself compelled to buy this kit to stop predators getting in, and by predators I don't mean foxes, wolves or bears, no, nothing like that. I mean Father bloody Frederick. He's a nightmare. Last year I had to get my favourite sheep out the river, well what was left of him, after our resident holy man ran him over while drink driving.

We thought that since he got married he'd sorted himself out, but he recently returned from his honeymoon and has since relapsed on the drink in a major way. He's already been heard falling about the village late at night, shouting out, 'I'm no longer a man.' I don't know if he's thinking about having a sex change or what, but whatever is happening, he is a deeply troubled and vulgar man.

I've bought this fence to put up around my cows as the other night I returned home from the cattle market to find him lying across one of my beasts; she was shaking from fear of what was happening to her. He was completely out of his face, and his socks and shoes were about ten feet away.

There being no love lost between us, I just pulled him down by the ankles and slung him over the fence into his own garden.

This will remind him to stay on his own side of the fence. Failing that, I'll order a handheld stun gun, which I heard is called a tazer or something.

-Farmer Bert

CASIO RETRO GOLD TONE DIGITAL WATCH A-168WG

Great for showing off how well you're doing.

About this time last year I was forced to leave the job I loved. I worked on the fair and lived a very good life. I won't go into it here, but it was a horrible experience and took me a while to recover. It still hurts to think, let along talk about. Luckily after I left the fair I was able to get a job (and a live-in sexual partner) at the pub in the village we were in when the unfortunate 'incident' that got me fired happened. Over the year that's passed I've come to build up a hatred for where I live, one much stronger than I had for the place when I only used to visit once a year, but I suppose living somewhere 24/7 365 days a year does that to a man.

The people here are OK; I mean, I hate one of them, but any chance I can get to make his life worse, I take and it makes me feel better.

However, hating Brian, the local spaz, wasn't going to make me feel better about all my old colleagues converging on the village come fair time. Living in a travelling family is very much about material items. When I'd had my own caravan to live in, it was full of all the best china, all the nicest accessories you could get put in when you bought it, it had everything you could want. Sadly I didn't own it, so couldn't take it with me; even if I had, the way the job ended, I doubt there would have been time.

So the time of year came when my former employers would

be with us and they'd be in the pub expecting me to serve them. I've spent pretty much 100 per cent of my wages on paying the endless tab I keep in the pub. Emma buys all the food and takes a bit out of my money before she gives it to me to put in the till, so I've nothing except a new jumper to show the family — that sacked me from the best job I've ever had — how much of a favour they did me by doing it. I was searching online to find something, anything, to show them when I came across this exquisite piece. Full gold all the way round. This and my Sta Press trousers were bound to impress them, or so I thought.

I thought to myself that when they got there, I'd be in the bar, looking great, rat tail tied tight, lights bouncing off the shiny watch and success oozing out of me. I probably wouldn't even need to say anything to them, they'd see me and realise what a mistake they'd made, beating the hell out of me last year. They'd remember how funny it was when I gave Brian the laxative-laden hotdogs. They might even offer me my old job back and I'd get to travel round meeting more women than the one that I've had to put up with for the last year. I'm not saying Emma is dull, but I'm a man of the world, I'm used to meeting hundreds of women through the summer. I hadn't been able to keep my title of sausage-hider of the year this time round and it pained me — not literally, but it made me feel less of a man to just have one woman.

On the first night the fair was in, they all bundled in the pub as soon as they arrived. The atmosphere was tense; there was still some bad blood on the side of the Driscoll family. They were still upset about one of the twins getting burnt with a cigarette.

Jeering, they were, making threats. I had to leave the bar in the hands of my woman on the first night. The watch was useless; they weren't prepared to notice it no matter now much I pulled my sleeve up and rubbed the watch shiny with my other cuff.

After the glass-throwing incident of the second night, I decided that the best thing to do was to meet with the head of the Driscoll family, John. So, donning a vest I borrowed from next door's line, I headed over there determined to put myself in a position where people would refrain from throwing glasses for long enough to see how much better I'd done in life without them.

The meeting didn't go well and I got home a few hours later, minus my watch, minus next door's vest and plus a few more bruises than I'd left the house with. Thinking about it, it might have been better just to shout it at them while dodging the glasses.

As soon as they're gone, I'm going to get Brian back for his part in this as it's pretty much all his fault I'm in this mess in the first place.

-Terry

CHINESE FIRECRACKER CACHETTE

These blow.

I was fairly sure that it was local simpleton who stole all my clothes. It was his flat I moved into. He was moved a few years ago due to him being a moron and not understanding that he can't sing at the top of his voice throughout the night, as neighbours don't tend to like that. From what Jock at the local pub told me, the council only rehomed him because he's 'special'. He got a house out of it, though, so once I've got more stuff, I think I might take up midnight karaoke too.

The flat was a right mess when I got here. Not having stuff to make it my own didn't help. I couldn't even clean it as all my cleaning stuff was in the suitcase that was stolen. It took a week for Social Services to pull their finger out and activate my 'emergency' setting up home grant.

I think Brian was jealous that I now had his old shag pad and he's holed up with ugly Janet with no chance of ever getting anyone else. I stalked him for a good couple of weeks, but he was never wearing my clothes. His cousin, who cuts his hair into a comb-over, wasn't either. It was too late though, I'd decided he was getting 'it' so I bought these crackers.

Rigging them up to go off on their own was a bit of an issue, but a couple of days hijacking the Wi-Fi at Father Frederick's meant I could research explosives and how to detonate them without fear of getting arrested for terrorism. I set his Wi-Fi up for him a couple of years ago at about 3 a.m.

and he's never changed the password since. I'm writing this review from outside his house now.

So with the crackers rigged to go off when Brian opens the door, I left and hedge-hopped over a couple more gardens to a) get away and b) find somewhere to watch the fun from.

I got bored in the end so I never got to see the explosion. I heard it, though. The whole village did. Wow! I knew it was a good idea to fix 15 large crackers together.

Booooooom!

-Denny

ECP SHEEPSKIN CLASSIC SADDLE

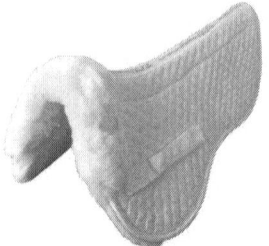

Perfect for not getting into a Buckaroo-type situation.

I hadn't ridden a cow since I was much younger; me and Bobby used to do it most weekends. We'd just stand on the stile, tempt them over by waving a handful of grass at them, and then when one was close enough, jump on and cling to it like our life depended on it. Which it did, actually. Cows don't really run that much unless they're scared, they're not co-ordinated enough. A quick tap in the belly with our heels was normally enough to set them off at a canter.

I've recently moved in on my own and Bobby's turned into a right square. I'm not really a drinker and was bored one day once Jeremy Kyle had finished. With there being only a pub and a Co-op to visit here, you need to, see, so I headed out to see what I could get up to in the village. I'm still trying to find out who stole all my clothes on the day I moved in, so seeing as it was a Monday I thought it would be a good idea to see if I could spot any of my stuff on other people's washing lines. After about ten minutes of looking, I got bored, though, and wandered off round the back of the vicarage; I thought Mary Woodford might be about and offer me some food. I couldn't see her though, and I wasn't going to knock on the door in case the old drunk, Father Frederick, answered. I wasn't interested in seeing him. That's when I saw the cows. They were in a different field to the one they used to be, electric fence too. We never had those round here when I was growing up or I absolutely guarantee that Bobby would have been thrown onto them on a regular basis. There was a wall to one side, though, and the cows were hanging about near it so I thought why not? It was bound to liven up my day. There was no one about except what looked like the guy from the pub who took a beating at the fair last year. He was in the distance walking and waving his arms about, so he wasn't going to say anything. He was clearly too busy having a breakdown.

So I jumped on the nearest beast. It made the same noise that cows always make when someone jumps on them, then just plodded about, I wanted to get my eye in a bit before I gave it a kick, I'm bigger than I used to be, so didn't want to get Buckaroo'd off.

Before I could, though, that complete idiot Frederick chucked a noise grenade into the field and my cow, along with the rest of them, bolted, charging towards the other end of the field with such urgency that I thought my time had come. I closed my eyes and did a 999 emergency prayer to the God I have never believed in. I could hear screaming and I couldn't tell you from that day to this if it was me or not. It was like I wasn't in full control or awareness. The buzz was amazing. If it wasn't for the fact I got hit with a shoe and taken to the ground I would have thoroughly enjoyed it. The shoe must have come from the same place as the alarm sound — unless the fence around the field was an alarm and not a normal electric fence.

What I do know is that however scared I was when the cow charged, I got such a rush of adrenaline from it that I am definitely doing it again. Although I won't do it without this saddle.

I've used it three or four times since and it performs every time, although I've never been able to get the same buzz as I did the first time. So I have to give the cow a good dig and then it goes. I suppose it's like drugs though, always chasing the first buzz.

If you need a saddle for riding cows, this is the one for you.

Getting it on and off could be easier, but thrill seekers can't have it all easy, can they?

-Denny

TRIXIE 30103 RUCKSACK FOR DOGS L 28 × 18 CM BLACK

You'll need to add a belt or two if you're attaching it to a cow.

As a secret drinker, I'm always looking for better places to hide my booze. Over the years I've been through all the regular places: wardrobes, toilet cisterns, in the shed, on the shed — everywhere. They all have one thing in common: the wife will always find them in the end. Well, it doesn't take much, does it? Just watch the drinker for a while and they'll lead you to it. I've accepted this is the case and the only way round it that I can think of is to hide a lot of it, everywhere, all the time. That way you'll always be able to find a drink when and as you need one.

Hence me buying this, although I don't own a dog and had no chance of catching one, they're all so fast. It wasn't for the want of trying, but I soon realised that the way you run when you're trying to catch a running dog is only going to lead to one thing, well a possible two: either I run into a car without seeing it, or I end up tripping over and grazing the tiny bits of nipple that I have left. I was in the garden with my afternoon litre of sherry pondering a solution when I realised it lay in front of me. Literally. The cows in the next field. *Cows are slow and pretty stupid, I'll have no problem getting this on them*, I thought to myself. Well, that wasn't strictly true. The strap isn't big enough for a beast so I had to nip into the house, dodging

Mary, my wife, and her hitting stick. I grabbed a couple of my belts and by hooking them together I managed to make the strap big enough to fit. Now cows aren't fast, but they ain't half stubborn buggers to fit a belt to. I bet that's why people from olden times never used them to ride on. The one I chose kept trying to wander off, there was no stopping him, I just had to work round the movement. It was thirsty work.

Finally I managed to get it on, although I'd finished the bottle I took with me by the time I did. The cow wandered off and sat down. I was fairly tired and leaned up against his friend who had got bored of watching and had the same idea as me: to have a sleep. I was woken up by an angry farmer a few hours later, screaming about how he needed protection and that I would be in for another accident with the mousetraps. I wasn't prepared to listen to his threats so went back into mine. Plus, if I'd hung about he'd have had more chance of seeing his cow's new accessories.

I've used the strap a couple of times. I think I'll stop using it regularly as it's just too much effort to get the drink, these cows have far too much freedom. The field they roam is huge and they've got no loyalty. I've had to spend over two hours finding the cow, pinning it down and removing my drink in the last couple of days. It's just not worth it. There's still a bottle with him, but I will try and leave it as an extra emergency bottle.

If you're thinking of using this for the same purpose as me, I'd suggest digging a hole instead. It's just easier to get your hands on your drink.

Nothing against cows myself, but I think the ones round here have something against me.

-Father Frederick

RAZOR E100 ELECTRIC SCOOTER — RED

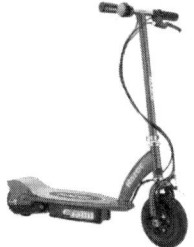

Not as fast as I thought it would be.

In return for getting him a job, my cousin Brian let me move into his place for the summer. I've lived at home too long and I needed to get some independence in my life. It was OK, though, as his wife, Janet, still cooked all my meals, bought all the bananas I could eat and washed my Westlife/Jackson Five collage T-shirt for me every other day, making sure it was fresh for the morning. Mother normally washes it once a week, but as I am travelling further to work, I sweat more, so it needs doing more often as Mr Hogsbottom, my boss, told me I was starting to smell like French onion soup.

Normally I wouldn't listen to him, but I was late that day, as I have been every day since I moved, so I felt it best to take on board what he was saying. Well, that and the fact it was true; under my arms smelled more European than the Eiffel tower.

I've never been able to pass the driving test; in fact, I've failed a miserable thirty-seven times. I've tried the lot: intensive courses, intense instructors. All the people that are in the Yellow Pages who claim to be able to get anyone through their test are liars. So travel has always been a problem. I don't mind walking, but walking fifteen miles a day is a bit much for even me. I don't have enough thoughts to keep me occupied for that long, even if I play the car colour counting game.

This scooter seemed the perfect answer. Now, it isn't that

slow when you go flat out, not fast enough to scare a man, but it's OK; the problem is if I go flat out at the eight mile an hour top speed, the battery wears out and dies halfway to work. In fact, it was after pushing it the other half of the way that I was told about my French onion aroma. So what I have to do is slow down to a measly three miles an hour; that way it gets to just outside the work gates. I then have to charge it up all day, which isn't enough for a full journey home and I end up I having to push it for a couple of miles back to the village. Sometimes it's more than a couple of miles as I have my Jackson Five/Westlife montage on as I ride. Music excites me, especially at the moments when Westlife turn up the pitch and jump off their stools for the finale of a song.

I've banned my cousin Brian from riding this scooter as he tried to jump it down the stairs near the Co-op and almost broke it. The brake is all funny now. I found out the hard way as I was riding out of the village one morning at 5 a.m. Some nutter in a Land Rover flew towards me on the wrong side of the road. I couldn't brake as the lever was jammed in 'off'. I had to head back to the village and borrow some TCP for my grazes before heading back to work.

I reported it to the local policeman, but he said he couldn't do anything because I was in the middle of the road on my scooter when, if anything, I should have been on the right side. I don't care what he says, though, I need to go in the middle of the road as I have no lights and the verge is too easy to crash into and you could find yourself at the bottom of a damp ditch with no one to pull you out of it until lunchtime. Mr Hogsbottom was not pleased that morning, I can tell you.

The only other thing I'd advise with this scooter is not to try and take two people on it. When I was on my way home one night I came across a drunk man with no shirt on. I offered him a lift as he seemed like he needed it. I shouldn't have, all the crying he was doing turned into hysterical wailing and he ended up pulling us both off the back of the scooter and into the road. As I left him to it, he was shouting 'It's happening again!' God only knows what he was talking about.

I've managed to get a replacement after telling the seller that the brake just 'fell' off when I was riding. I'm more careful with the replacement.

-Jeff

DOMESTOS BLEACH ORIGINAL 750ML

Good turnip killer.

So it was that mad old bint, Ethel, who nicked all my stuff when I moved into the flat. It's taken me all summer to find it and to be honest I only found it by accident. I was hedge-hopping away from Brian's house after leaving a nice surprise for him, in his shed. Well, up until then it was only Brian that I thought would have had reason to steal my bag. If I didn't hate Brian with everything I have in my soul, I'd have gone back and removed his 'gift' but I do, so I didn't.

The clothes were ruined and in a pile, wet and completely unwearable. All my porn mags were gone, too, I bet she took them in for her nutty old man or something. The dirty old cow had started making some vile compost next to the pile of clothes and rather than kick down her plants, which is something I would have done when I was younger, I needed to do something worse. Much worse.

Now, I'm not in the market for letting people take liberties with me so I needed a plan. It took some Internet searching, but I found a website, Beatingthejones.com, which seemed specifically made for helping you ruin your neighbour's garden. It didn't take long to find the item suggested.

This stuff worked a treat. I poured it about a hundred times more liberally than the label suggested, I could almost see smoke rising up out of the compost. The thick white crust that makes everything die appeared almost instantly. When I think back I wished I'd chucked some of the bleach on Brian's garden, too, it might have killed them stupid chickens that he takes for walks in the village. They wouldn't be able to wake me up at stupid o'clock, then.

All I have to do now is sit back and Ethel will kill her own plants and veg. The plan is flawless.

Maybe if I'm really lucky she'll end up eating some of it. A week on the toilet passing bleach would really show her.

The only downside of all this, apart from losing all my clothes, of course, is that I won't be able to let the old bag know that it was me who ruined her garden.

The bleach isn't bad at getting muck out of carpets, either; someone was sick through my letterbox. Don't worry, though, I'll get them back for it.

-Denny

TWO-TONE CLASSIC COVER: JEREMIAH 29 [LEATHER BOUND]

A good gift to remind people not to stray (to any other religion).

It's so great to have someone who wishes to convert to Christianity. I've known young Bobby for a number of years now, he used to be in with a bad lot, but now he's come over to the flock of the living Lord, Jesus Christ.

Being a Bishop, I've not had much 'hands on' work for the last few years. I manage the vicars and make sure they're not doing anything they shouldn't be, which is more work than you'd think managing a load of God's men should be. The age old saying is 5 per cent of your employees cause 95 per cent of the problems. And one of my more rural vicars is that 5 per cent. I thought we'd managed to sort him out, I thought him getting the woman he's been obsessed with for thirty years would be the thing to change him. It's not, though, and the worst thing is, I can't get rid of him until he does something really bad. Alcoholism being an illness these days makes it impossible to do anything but medically retire him, but if I was to do that, due to Church rules, I have to give him the house he lives in and let him stay there as long as he wants. That would be great, if I didn't lose complete control of him through that path.

Anyway, that is the backdrop to the wonderful

transformation that I am not privy to watching. If Father Frederick wasn't such a nightmare, I wouldn't have been blessed with seeing young Bobby turn his life around. He decided a while ago that throwing things at old people and knocking on doors before running away wasn't a good path in life. We were able to engage him through the Youth Club and since then he's done Bible study after Bible study, he's fully immersed himself into the life of a proper Christian and even agreed to make amends to some of the local residents for his past behaviour and promised to help them wherever possible in the future.

I've bought him this Bible cover as a reward for being such a good Christian. Also, so everyone knows he's on my firm and not any of the other, wrong religions. My God is the only one that should be worshipped and Bobby understands that. This book cover will make sure he NEVER, NEVER forgets it.

-Bishop Desmond

ST JOHN AMBULANCE FABRIC PLASTERS — 100-PACK

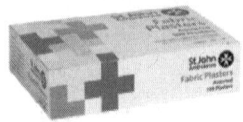

Good for unexplained scratches.

I feel like I need a never-ending supply of these in my house. My husband is forever coming home with scrapes and cuts. He's a lovely bloke, but he really has no sense of danger. In fact that's putting it too kindly; he has no common sense. Lovely guy, but fairly thick, if I'm honest.

There was no explanation for the last lot of cuts; I don't know what he'd been doing, but he looked like he'd been attacked by the chickens again. He didn't want to talk about it, though, and turned the TV up loud so I couldn't ask him any more questions while I nursed his arms, legs and stomach with these plasters. He wouldn't let me put a plaster on his head, though.

If he wasn't so ugly and useless with women, I might think he'd been up to something else; but, seeing as he'd only been with a woman that he'd made out of pillows before me, I don't think I've got anything to worry about on that front.

-Janet

GORILLA TAPE 11M

Does the job.

I recently found myself in need of a good tape. I came home and someone had thrown something at my window so hard it had cracked all the way down the middle. The council only came and put the double glazing in a couple of years ago so you can imagine how furious I was. I was straight round to the idiot's next door to find out exactly what he'd done this time. You see, it wasn't more than a week ago that he crushed my wheelie bin, so I was sure it was him. I was trying to get the simpleton's attention by banging on the door. I knew he was in; I could hear him shouting out one of Barry White's songs in the monotone that he thinks is singing. I had to wait a full song for him to be able to hear the door. When he opened it, I challenged him about the latest bit of vandalism. He swore it wasn't him and even came out to inspect the damage. I still think it was him, though, as he picked up a bit of metal from under the window and told me that was the likely cause of it. It was like a hook or something. He wouldn't admit it, though, and I sent him back inside before his belligerence made me angry.

    I called the council and reported the repair, but they said they wouldn't come and fix it until I'd rung the police and got a crime reference number. So until I do that and wait the likely fifteen years for them to bother coming out and looking at the crack, I've stuck a bit of this tape over it to keep the heat in and the cold out. It's worked well. Although I shouldn't have taped it quite so much as I can't open either this window or its twin, opposite it.

Never mind, at least I'm not cold. I hate being cold.

-Margaret Copperfield

DUREX ELITE CONDOMS — 12 PACK

More than one use.

I like a ramble now and then. Me and Nature are friends. Well, I need to be friends with Nature or I'd have even fewer friends in this world. So walking is something I've always enjoyed. I get to sing while I'm out, too, and I love singing.

Never in my time living in the countryside have I needed to worry about finding a Portaloo to relieve myself in. Unfortunately things are changing in this modern world we live in. I was recently out on my regular Tuesday evening walk. Being someone who abides by the Country Code, I will never get little Frank out when someone could see him and get scared. I ALWAYS find a fence to let the dirty water flow out of my body against. It's just polite. I did just that on this particular Tuesday. Now, I know that everything is digital these days, e-reader, e-cigarettes, e-everything. I really didn't think it would make it out to the country, though. E-fences. I mean who makes a fence electric and why? It's ridiculous. Unfortunately I didn't realise it was electric until the current travelled up the stream of man wee and connected a direct hit with my tenders. Apparently the shock is doubled if it's channelled through liquid. I was thrown at least three feet backwards into a bramble bush.

In the half an hour it took me to come round, no one found me. I was dreaming that I was in bed, which made waking up even more terrifying. There were thorns everywhere, I was even clutching some, just like I do with the corner of the quilt when I'm actually in bed, which is where I usually do my sleeping. Being as no one was there to help I had to get out myself. I tried just standing up, but that just got me a load of thorns in the top of my head so I wriggled out on my back, like a worm. This caused my jumper to get caught on a thorn and ride up. By the time I was out, my torso, arms and face were scratched to hell.

I've decided from now on that I'm going to take these condoms out with me and use them to pass my water into. Then I'll tie the top, put them in a carrier bag and flush them away once I get home.

The world is a much sadder place in 2013 than I ever thought it would be.

I suppose they'll have to update the Country Code now.

-Brian

SENNHEISER HD201 LIGHTWEIGHT OVER-EAR BINAURAL HEADPHONES

Less boring than ear plugs.

I swear there are some weirdos round my way. The simpleton next door seems to have gone quiet recently. Thank the Lord. He's got a wife now and isn't singing along to the TV theme tunes anymore, I don't think she lets him. With the peace I was getting I threw away my ear plugs, something which I now consider one of the biggest mistakes of my life. Even more so than not wearing clean pants on the day that I tripped over, fell off the bus and had to be hospitalised. I still don't know where those pants ended up. I know where the ear plugs went, though: in the bin, that's where. Brian became the least of my problems, though, as I was hearing the couple at the pub having arguments long after closing. Really going at it, they were. Then there was some very strange screaming in the street. It was from a male, and at first I thought it was Terry and Emma having another barney, but this was closer, the voice was right outside my window. It frightened me to death. The man was shouting, 'I'm no longer a man, God has taken away my need for me to own nipples,' or something like that. I've read in the news that there are more of these paedophiles around these days. I'm not sure what they are, exactly, but they sound like a right nightmare, into weird sex things, so I assume this person was one. I'd hoped it was just a travelling one, but unfortunately a couple of nights later, the same thing. Then the frequency became more and more until I eventually had to look into getting some more ear plugs. Although while I was searching, I came across the gadget I've been waiting years for: these ear muffs that have tiny little speakers in. This is great as it means my dream of ear plugs and music can't be too far away.

I plugged the musical ear muffs into my wireless and listened to the shipping forecast on full volume the first night. Since then I've gone to sleep listening to all manner of different radio. There is a late night love show on the local radio where teenagers ring in and pretend they are grown up with grown up issues. It's nice to listen to young love. It's also nice that I don't have to listen to one of those paedophiles shouting outside my window anymore, too.

-Margaret Copperfield

AIRWALK BUTTON V-NECK KNITTED JUMPER MEN'S

Comfortable on the nips.

I had to buy a new jumper. I needed it quick and living in an isolated village, the options for obtaining new jumpers are either theft from washing lines, which gives a very limited choice round here, or ordering online.

I can hear you asking why I would need a new jumper so urgently: I'll tell you. I recently went into the local town after a new microwave for the kitchen of the pub I work in. I decided to keep the money I was given by my boss (and girlfriend) and was planning just to pick up a microwave and run out the fire escape with it. Which I did, but as I got out the door, I slipped on something and fell flat on my back. At first I thought someone had chucked a tin of paint down the stairs, but as I was limping away as quick as I could, I started to notice that my back stunk like the pub toilets do on Sambuca night. Which means vomit, for all of you out there that haven't attended one of my Mexican evenings.

I had to strip there and then if I was to get away without being poleaxed by a bout of vomiting myself. Luckily when I'd slipped I'd let go of the microwave box and it landed back in the store, so no crime had been committed and the police wouldn't have been called. Good job, too — who needs arresting when they're topless and wearing only purple Sta Press trousers, limping like they've just left the prison showers.

I've only ever had one good jumper and the T-shirt I

owned had been stolen off the line when the fair was here. Me working behind the bar with my chest on full display wasn't something that would have gone down well, it would have definitely caused someone to write 'Terry is a bender' on the toilet wall again.

This one had a nice pattern and the delivery came as promised. I just wish that I'd ordered the replacement T-shirt on the same timescale, as the jumper alone is a little itchy. It makes my nipples sore.

If, like me, you own one jumper and no T-shirt, when working, don't rub ice cubes on your nipples to soothe them; someone will go into your toilets and question your sexuality in permanent marker on the wall.

-Terry

HOW TO BE ASSERTIVE IN ANY SITUATION [PAPERBACK]

Learn to stand up for yourself!

I got this book to read to my cousin. I've recently moved in with him and I soon discovered all the stories he used to tell me about how he is well-liked in the village and how he gets up to all sorts of adventures are all lies. He's made them up. It turns out almost everyone hates him. I've always been a man to keep myself to myself. I like The Jackson Five, Westlife and half-bananas. I've never been really interested in much else. I won't allow anyone to take liberties with me, though. Just ask the people I work with, they saw the fact that I cut my hair into a comb-over as a sign of weakness and an opportunity to mock me, especially the resident witch, Sheila. Well, I soon taught them and I didn't even need this book. I fed the seagulls laxatives and let them do their business on everyone's car/head/sandwiches.

So for me to find out I'm related to such a wimp wasn't so much hard to swallow, more saddening. I'd believed he was living a great life here in the country, that's why I moved here. It just wasn't the case though.

I decided I needed to do something about it when there was a karaoke night in the Lamb and Whistle and Brian wouldn't agree to go, as someone called Jock had thrown him out the pub before. Now, it took me a little while to get the information out of Brian. He seems to have pushed a lot of incidents of what I can see as good old-fashioned bullying to the bottom of his subconscious and it's just easier for his own well-being if he doesn't think about them. I can't have the best singer in the house not being able to have the chance to be the best singer in the pub. I'm sure none of The Jackson Five ever let someone who doesn't even work at a pub throw them out of it.

That's where this book comes in. I decided that I was going to teach Brian to be assertive. You don't need to be violent to be able to dissuade someone from pushing you around and telling you what to do. As proved by me with the seagulls.

I read the book out loud to Brian and we went over eye contact, saying things in a nice way and basically dealing with the fear of the unknown; i.e. Brian hasn't known that Jock is more than likely to be all mouth and trousers. Most bullies are.

The night came, as they have a tendency to do. I sported my favourite T-shirt, Brian put on his full Barry White uniform and we headed over to the pub armed with nothing but our new found assertiveness. Well, that and a few laxatives to slip in Jock's drink just as a way of getting him back.

It started as soon as we walked in. Jock was eyeing us up, trying to catch Brian's eye. He didn't like it when Brian wouldn't look at him. I made sure I kept Brian smiling, just to send the message to Jock that we wouldn't be intimidated. The barman kept us busy explaining why he was only wearing one shoe; well he did until he was sent upstairs by his boss for not being appropriately dressed for work.

We put our names in for the second song. I don't really like singing, but decided I would stand there moving my mouth like a wet fish, just to show my cousin some solidarity. Once we got back to our table, it was time for Jock to shift his gears to idiot factor twelve and approach us.

Now there's a time for assertiveness and then there's a time for cock punches, and someone calling your cousin a 'complete and utter cow pat' is definitely a time for a cock punch. I drew back like a pro, the snap was like something you'd learn in the army. If you were in the army. I learnt it off YouTube and practised it on the internal doors at my mother's house, but more about why I don't live there anymore later. Back to Jock: at first it looked like he was going to ride the storm. All I could think to do was draw back and let another one of the now famous cock punches go. The second one seemed to bring him back into the land of the living; before he'd just been swaying and doing some strange eye movements. Scary enough, but when someone starts jumping up and down and howling like a beast, it's worse. The man must be fairly hard. I've never seen anyone take two full on cock punches and stay standing. Jock did, though.

I must have trained Brian well as he had a go at doing the same. His wasn't as effective as mine, in fact it was the opposite of being effective. It got him a slap in the chops. It must have stung, the slap echoed round the pub. I thought that it was all going to go wrong, but just then, years of being mistreated, years of being shouted at in the street, at having his personal possessions stolen, broken or having nasties smeared on them all came out. Brian leapt at Jock. I didn't think I'd see the day. To be honest, I didn't think I'd need to, such was my faith in cock punching. I did, though. I saw Brian bite, kick and hair-pull his way into the higher appreciation of the whole pub. Jock went down when Brian slapped him like you would a newborn that wasn't breathing. He just kept slapping, giving him one with the palm of his hand one way then the back of his hand on the backswing, then repeating at record speed. To be honest it was probably the most girlie revenge beating that has ever been dished out. Effective though. Jock called time out from the floor, although it took me pulling Brian away for the spitting to stop. He was raging.

Jock was helped to his feet and made a sharp exit. I expected him to return with a lead pipe or something, but he didn't.

The strangest thing was that like a switch being flipped, Brian swapped back to his old self and was singing Barry White, on his own and in front of everyone, within five minutes of what had just happened.

If you're a bit of a sad bullied wretch, I'd recommend this book and a pep talk from your cousin, followed by an example of when cock punching is appropriate, Then you'll be able to deal with anyone.

Great book. Although I am returning it for a refund, I'm not made of money and Brian is sorted now, I don't need this book for me, I can cock punch at will.

-Jeff

RECYCLE BIN SLATE/GREEN 50L

Not as good as the Council ones, but OK.

I don't know what happened to my Council owned bin, but I came out of my house one morning and it was squashed flat. There was no fixing it, either — I tried. The Council claim that bins don't just fall over and collapse in on themselves and that I am responsible for the care of my bin. Anything that gets them out of helping people, my Council will do. They're a disgrace. I asked what I should do about a replacement and they stopped short of suggesting I steal one from someone else's garden, but that's the feeling I got. So I did just that, but unfortunately for me, I was seen taking it and when I denied doing it the true owner pointed to her door number that she'd scratched onto the handle. I suppose she's had her bin nicked before. There was no other option (other than paying the £200 the Council wanted for a replacement) than to buy my own.

This one is OK. I managed to fit my old recycling bin in it, although it took a little cutting and bending of the plastic.

When the rubbish men came they refused to take it, telling me it was a bin for inside the house. I told them my predicament and they promised to bring me one from one of the empty houses.

All in all this was a little bit of a waste of money, but on the plus side I can now keep all my wet cardboard and empty bottles in the house. I might see if I can get some wheels on it so I can wheel it outside to empty it.

-Margaret Copperfield

DRAPER EXPERT 57768 190MM WIRE ROPE AND WIRE CUTTERS

They certainly cut.

I like to keep a variety of tools in my shopping cart when I'm out walking, just in case I come across something that takes my fancy and it is bolted down. Or there's a fence a bit too high for me to climb over, or too long to walk around. I lost my last set of tools when my old trolley exploded.

These came along with some other tools and I immediately put them in the trolley ready for my next walk.

I went out later that day; I was dying to try out my new cutters. Once I'd visited the bins near the Co-op I could wait no longer and right there in front of me was the perfect opportunity: a BMX bike, and BMX bikes have wires on them that are just begging to be cut. So that's what I did. I have to say these Draper cutters were keen as mustard. They went through the wires in one go and didn't even leave the slightest mark on my fingers where I squeezed.

I've since cut all sorts of things with them: wire fences, car aerials, handbag straps, they'll cut anything within reason. They also don't squeak like the last lot I had. I've vowed to keep these ones inside so they never get old or rusty.

I wish I could say the same for me.

-Ethel

MR MEN SOCKS 3 PACK MEN'S

You don't just get one pair, you get three!

I've never had three pairs of socks before. During vicar college, they only issued one pair and I was so used to spending my allowance on secret sherry that I never bothered to buy more than one pair. I got used to buying secret sherry with my wages too, so I just wash the pair I have at the end of the week.

Last week, though, I got home after some secret sherry drinking, well, I found myself in the garden, and I'd misplaced my socks. The good Lord has yet to reveal where they got to, so I've had to buy some more. This three pack cost less than half a bottle of sherry, so I was able to justify the expenditure, and I just had a morning on the communal wine instead, so you could say the socks cost me nothing at all. They're really comfortable, too. I recently had a pretty horrible accident and my feet were a little bruised as a result. These feel like I'm walking on clouds compared to my old pair, which felt like I was walking on sandpaper.

Maybe I should steal the church wine more often so I can afford these little luxuries in life.

-Father Frederick

AMSCAN PINATA BAT

A good whacking stick.

I bought this for the Youth Club, they like a varied and fun activity list. It keeps them interested in attending and out of trouble.

However, due to the ongoing problem of my husband being a complete drunk moron, I've decided to keep this hitting stick at home. He's still pretending that he's sober even though he drinks to blackout most days, and when he's drunk tells me he's relapsed, but by the morning he's back to hiding it.

Every single night he comes home in a state. Crawling from the car to the house, due to his recent accident things are worse, it's like he's given up. He damaged his man zones during our honeymoon and feels that the thirty years he spent stalking me are wasted now as he can't consummate the relationship. He seems to have forgotten that during the honeymoon, before the accident he couldn't do that anyway as he was too drunk. But we work with what we've got and while I wait to make sure that I am entitled to half of everything he's got, I'm his maid. His maid who beats him with this stick to wake him up from the lawn in the middle of the night to make sure he isn't spread-eagled there when the neighbours wake up in the morning.

It's a great motivator, this stick, and if you stick to shins and knees, it barely leaves a mark. He doesn't even know he was passed out on the lawn most days.

If you need a good hitting stick then this is the kiddie. It gets the results you want without too much marking. Although I can't guarantee it would be a good stick for children, as they bruise easier; probably best to use a slipper or rubber mallet for them.

-Mary Woodford

WOODEN COMPOSTER LARGE

I never knew clothes could be used as compost.

I used to use my recycling bin for compost; however, it went missing and my husband said he saw the bin men taking it away. My husband is fairly mad these days so I'm not sure whether he really saw that or he did something with it himself and can't remember. The long and short of it was, though, it was gone and I needed to think outside the box if I was going to get a new one. The council wouldn't replace it even if I asked. They've been writing to me for years demanding that I stop using it for compost. I didn't think they'd take it away, though. I'm almost glad I smeared the rim of the lid with dog dirt now.

Being a keen gardener and a keener forager, I'm always on the look out for things that can improve my turnip crop. I was also told that it was Denny, the local tearaway that blew up my old shopping cart by catapulting a banger into it last year. So it was with some joy that I found a suitcase full of clothes and some 'art' magazines right outside Brian's old flat, which Denny was moving into. I had to be quick to get it away but thankfully it was on wheels, so if you think about it, God wanted this to happen. I'd have never been able to carry it without the wheels. Denny deserves to be punished and even God knows it.

I put most of the clothes under a bit of tarpaulin with some mud and water, and the rest I've chopped up and left in the suitcase along with some eggs, soil and various leaves.

The suitcase didn't last long and disintegrated within a month. I'd have thought it would have lasted longer, but it didn't. When I looked inside, though, the compost was the best I've ever produced. It smelled great; a thin white topping is the sign of a good compost and this load had a thick top. I was really excited to get it on the turnips.

First I had to transfer it to this new box, though, and so far it's held up better than the suitcase did. (Although I did just leave the bits that were left of the suitcase in the compost mix.)

I'm glad I was gifted the joy of compost and revenge. Some people judge me for the way I conduct myself, but like someone, somewhere said, only God can judge me and I am OK with that. I'll take him some turnips when my time comes, then if there is anything he's upset with, the grade A turnips will smooth things over.

-Ethel

MAVERICK FLAT SLIP ON SHOE / TASSEL TRIM VAMP

Top tassels AND cheap!

Things haven't been good in my life lately. The guys I used to work for coming back into my village and my life for a week didn't help. The relationship I'm in won't stand much more of me stealing her alcohol and money, and I lost my new watch in a game of cards. Mr Driscoll said on his last night that we could play poker for my dignity. If I won, they would allow me to be in the same village as them and not get taunted. If I lost I had to give them everything of value that I had on me. The watch was it. They didn't want my old purple Sta Press trousers, which was more an insult than a relief. I love those trousers.

I needed to leave the village immediately. Well, at least make it look like I was leaving, so I headed off over the fields. It was nice just to get out in the air, it's hard to remember what fresh air smells like when you've spent years working at the fair, full of petrol and fried onions, then go straight into a pub.

Unfortunately I didn't get to enjoy the peace for long as someone's burglar alarm started going off, which isn't a surprise with my ex friends in town. I ignored it and tried to walk away from the noise. I thought the weather was turning as I started to hear thunder. It wasn't though. It was worse. I turned round to see a herd of cows charging towards me with no signs of slowing down. I've heard of mad cow disease but I thought it was just a nickname for the burgers at the fair. These ones must have been really mad. I didn't even know they could move that fast. I had to think quick and there was only one outcome of my quick thinking: I ran, and I ran fast.

I lost one of my shoes somewhere as I sprinted to the gate. I'm not sure whereabouts it went and I only realised once I was halfway across the next field and had to stop to throw up. But I sure as hell wasn't going back in that field so I had to hang about all evening in the woods until I could sneak back into the pub without being seen by Mr Driscoll.

These little beauties are OK, they go well with my Sta Press trousers. And they have all the tassels. I'd lost some on my old shoes. The best thing is that Emma, my girlfriend, paid for them on her credit card; she said she couldn't have a boyfriend that only had one shoe to his name.

Now I've got three shoes, she is more than happy to let me see her in the nude again and I like nude. Women, not men. I'm not into blood sausage.

I'd recommend these shoes to anyone, I imagine they'd go with anything: Sta Press trousers, a suit, joggers ... they're versatile ... AND you get to see breasts if you wear them.

-Terry

HONK IF YOUR HORNY FUNNY BUMPER STICKER CAR VAN BIKE STICKER DECAL FREE P&P

HONK!
IF YOUR HORNY

A perfect sign for a wind up.

Having been behaving myself for a while, I felt the need to get into some mischief and the perfect person to target is Father Frederick. He's a bit dim, and seeing as how it was his stupidity that put me in jail last year, it's him that was due to get this sticker glued to his car. He's recently got a new one and seeing as how he's drinking again, there was no way he'd be able to see it.

The glue was super-sticky, he'd lose his fingernails long before he got the sticker off.

The sticker came quickly and the same night I was waiting for Father Frederick to crawl out of his car and put himself into bed, either where he lay or in the house, depending on how much he'd been hitting the church sherry that day. As it turned out, he made it into the house. Doing a professional job of it, I wiped all the dead bugs off the bumper with some white spirit, then dried it with my sleeve and held the sticker on tight for a good couple of minutes to make sure it was attached properly.

I've seen him driving about a few times since, although I haven't witnessed anyone honking him.

It'll happen though, I'm sure of it.

-Denny

SILVERLINE BUNGEE CORDS 6PK

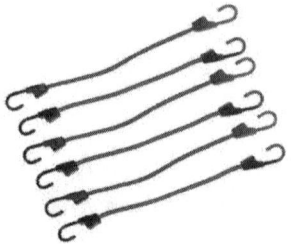

Good ties.

I've tried everything to hide bottles of booze. These are my latest effort. I used them to strap three bottles under the carriage of my Mini. If you're thinking of doing the same, I would recommend you only go on motorway journeys. With all the bumps and hills around my village it didn't really work. Not only did I lose the bottles, I also lost a couple of the straps. I suspect that once the bottle was gone, the cord went slack and unhooked itself. I've started to use the remaining straps to keep bottles secure on the roof of the shed.

-Father Frederick

Great for tying things closed.

These are great. I found a couple by the side of the road on one of my walks. I was planning on using them to keep the larger items I find strapped to my shopping trolley, which comes everywhere with me, but then I got a better idea. I was on my way home that day when I looked over and spotted Denny, the little swine who put bangers in my last trolley, in the phone box. I got a better idea of what to use them for then. The silly little sod was engrossed in some little book as I crept up, so I was able to attach the two cords together and wrap them round without him noticing. It was a tight stretch, but they held well. It exhausted me, but was worth it.

What happened next was brilliant, it couldn't have gone better. By the time I'd hidden myself away in the alley across the road I was able to see Denny struggling to get out. The cords held extra-tight and I could see him pushing with his legs against the door and his back against the actual phone unit. The door only opened a little when he pushed. I am really impressed with how much pressure the cords took before they ultimately snapped and flew off. Denny collapsed to the ground, catching the small of his back right on the step of the phone box. I watched him limp off home before going to collect the cords for my original use. One of them had broken, the metal end had come off and it wasn't lying around, either, so I'll have to think of another use for it.

These are great for attaching things, and locking little gits in phone boxes.

-Ethel

BLOMUS 68169 GREENS PLANT SPRAYER 0.3 L

A great firearm!

My boss is a pretentious git. He won't have the standard plastic bottle that bleach or toilet cleaner comes in. He likes to have metal ones and he gets me, his cleaner, to empty them out of the bottle they come in and into these. Makes no difference to me unless it's winter as they get cold and are harder to hold then, so if he wants to make sure people think he's special and different and continue to pay me for transferring liquid from one bottle to another, then so be it.

He even makes us put doilies under the bottles if we put them down. Most cleaners carry around dusters in their pinny pockets; not us, we carry travel doilies. There are very few perks to being a cleaner for 'Lord' Monty. One we do have, though, is taking the cleaning products home and using them in our own houses.

I was just popping through the woods to take the cleaning fluid over to my colleague Mary's house the other day when my dog became all alert, his ears pricked up and he looked at me for permission to attack. I couldn't see what the problem was at first. I soon did, though, there was some old pervert standing in the hedge. I could only see his eyes, so, remembering that a policeman once tried to tell me that his pathetic pepper spray was a firearm, I decided I'd use my 'firearm' and aimed for his peepers with this. I got a bull's eye into both of the dirty swine's peepers. I was away before he hit the ground, but I could hear him screaming as I went. Reminded me of most mornings when that idiot Monty gets shower gel in his eyes.

I saw Chopper, the gamekeeper who hates Monty more than any of the staff, on the way out of the woods, and he said there'd been a lot of screaming in the woods lately.

Still, thankfully I had this bottle with me and the spray action kept me safe.

Even if you just use it for water, I'd recommend it. Just go easy when you spray as this one pushes the liquid out fast.

-Molly the cleaner

GREEN MOSAIC LIZARD RESIN GARDEN ORNAMENT

Great for fooling fools.

This really is a nice looking piece. The daft old sod I work for is so gullible, the other week he even bought a Lordship off the Internet. He thinks that no one knew he wasn't a real Lord; everyone does, though. There are Internet sites set up purely to mock him and his stupid family. I know, because I set most of them up. It's only because some great, great, great grandfather of his was a bit of a nutcase in the dark ages and pretty much owned York that there is still any money left. Monty will present himself to be ripped off at any given opportunity. Since that nutter from York started sleeping with his granddaughter things have gone from bad to worse for this family. I think one of them is even the Chancellor of the Exchequer at the moment. Still all rich, but stupid as hell.

This piece was cheap enough for me to afford from my wages, but looks old enough to pass off as something someone famous would have touched, owned or sat on at one time or another. Monty loves to buy things he thinks I've stolen out of other rich, stupid people's houses. I'm more than happy to oblige. Once I even sold him the same clock twice. He thinks he has one in the guest bedroom and one in his study, but keeps forgetting he moved it. Such is his trust in anyone that smiles at him.

I gave him this after a shoot that was local, on the land that connects to ours. There was the usual banter between him and the other landowner about who got to keep the birds and which land they'd taken off from. Monty and Harold always argue and Monty is more than happy to think that I've been into Harold's home and stolen his things while they're shooting. So I bought this well in advance of us going that Sunday morning. It was in the Land Rover on the way home that I presented it to him. He reminded me to keep my eyes on the road as we'd nearly knocked someone off their bike on the way there earlier that morning. But apart from that, he was pleased as punch and fully believed that it was once owned by Joan of Arc.

I don't know why he does it because he can't tell anyone he has these things, he just likes to tell me about it. It's like a weird game. He knows they're nicked, I know they're cheap tat, but that doesn't stop him telling me complete nonsensical stories about how they came to be in his family.

I suppose the three thousand pounds he pays me per item also includes an 'audience fee', which I can't really moan about, can I?

-Chopper

PATRIOT HIGH FREQUENCY PERSONAL ATTACK ALARM WITH BRIGHT TORCH 130+DB

Keeps perverts at bay but don't lose the nib.
This is my second alarm; I'll explain what happened to the first later. I bought this alarm as I keep being followed by what can only be described as perverts, beeping their horns and waving at me, asking me to pull over. It's very off putting when you're trying to drink drive.

You might ask how I know they're perverts; well I'll tell you: the first time it happened, I thought I must have a problem with my car, a flat tyre or something, so I got out and thanked the guy for stopping. I shouldn't have, as I walked up to the window I thought he was cleaning a knife with his hanky or something, it turned out he was doing something far more ungodly. He was shouting something, but I didn't stop.

It must have been the brandy, but I'd forgotten about it when later that week someone else was beeping me and pulling me over. I stopped, keen to see what the issue was; this chap got out the car and made me the sort of offer that I haven't heard since boarding school. Although I wouldn't do anything like that these days and not for anything less than a full bag of Haribo, anyway, (to take the taste away). This one was persistent, though, and I had to drive round the ring road of the local town seventeen times before he got bored of following me and I was able to go home.

It must be some sort of strange Internet craze or

something, 'follow a vicar' or something like that. Either way, the noise this little beaut produces will stop them playing with their ding-a-ling in front of me.

This alarm helped somewhat when the latest person to pull me over actually got out holding his teeny weeny in his hand; the alarm has a good sound to it, so good in fact that along with scaring the filthy work of the devil away it also sent me a little dizzy.

I'd also suggest to anyone who buys this to not let it off in your own house. I did this as soon as the parcel arrived. As it was morning, I hadn't dealt with my shakes and I couldn't get the plug back in to switch it off. My wife was screaming down the stairs asking if we were being burgled or if I'd set fire to the kitchen again. I managed to get my secret brandy out from under the sink and belt down a few gulps, but by the time I got back to the table where I'd left the alarm, I'd lost the plug. It was getting to the point of making me feel sick and Mary had taken to slamming the door upstairs, it must have been sending her crazy.

The only thing I could think of to do was to chuck it outside, so I tried that. The window wasn't open, though, and it just bounced off and went under the table. I'm not mad enough to think these little things have minds of their own, but the good Lord must have been punishing me for something as it positioned itself at the furthest possible point it could, in the far corner against the back wall. I had to move all the heavy chairs out the way, then lie on the floor to get it. Getting up was harder than getting down and holding the alarm close to my head just made things even worse. Once I'd managed to stagger to my feet I ran, tripped over some weird stick thing that I've never seen before, ripped my cassock and got to the door all within about three seconds. Once the door was open I threw it as far as I could. It landed somewhere in the farmer's field next door. I've read before that cows can't hear high pitched noises, though, so I was confident I'd ended the problem without causing anyone else any, which is God's way if you think about it.

I went back later to find it, but it was nowhere to be seen. I think the cows might have eaten it or something. It wasn't there when I got back from Aldi though.

-Father Frederick

MAGIC: THE COMPLETE COURSE (BOOK & DVD)
[PAPERBACK]

A waste of money.

I don't know why, but there is always shoes in the hedges round here. If I could sell single shoes I'd make a fortune. They are the one thing that I just throw straight on the fire. There's just nothing you can do with that single shoe. I was taking my new coat for a test run last week and found another, which I burnt, too. That's when I thought about magic ... I mean, that's the only thing that can truly bring things back from being burnt, isn't it?

Unfortunately this book doesn't tell you how to unburn things. I thought a book that taught magic would have at least one trick for this.

I don't normally want to unburn things that I've set fire to, but Terry from the pub had put a load of posters up looking for his missing shoe. I tried presenting him with the old Wellington I found in the hedge just behind the pub, but he wasn't interested in that. Just my luck that the one time I find a shoe that's worth £5 I burn it quicker than I normally would. It's my own fault for being excited about my new matches.

If you want real magic, you need to look further than Amazon — maybe witches or something — but this book just appears to show magic up for being tricks. We all know that's rubbish, though; real magic exists, just not on Amazon.

I've returned for a refund, I hope they don't notice I kept the DVD.

-Ethel

ESCAPING NORTH KOREA: DEFIANCE AND HOPE IN THE WORLD'S MOST REPRESSIVE COUNTRY
[PAPERBACK]

I'm a shivering denizen, too!

Now, I don't claim to have half the problems of those in North Korea. In fact my problems pale into insignificance when compared to them. I'd give up living if I was forced to have a haircut like them. However, I do understand what it's like to be trapped and forced into loving someone you actually don't like very much, so I thought this book would suit me down to the ground.

I spent years avoiding the man who was to become my husband. He basically stalked me into submission, lied to me about giving up drinking and then married me. I think he just wore me down. It's a horrible feeling being trapped in a marriage that I'd rather be leaving. He's a man of the cloth, his boss married us last year, so I doubt divorce is an option.

It's funny, when you're being manipulated you know it's happening, but you're powerless to stop it ... well, I was, anyway. It's like I've been under a spell.

I bought this book to see what sort of thing the defectors of North Korea have done to get away. I don't think I'll do anything as drastic as setting myself on fire, although I might set him on fire if he carries on coming home with bits of his clothing missing.

I read the book and it all seemed to be about actual escape, like running away and stuff. I thought there might be a bit more in it about escaping mentally while still living there; unfortunately, I don't really want to run away and even if I did, my own house is only up the road so he'd find me in no time.

I suppose I'll have to find a more specific book.

-Mary Woodford

THE RIGHT WAY TO KEEP CHICKENS [PAPERBACK]

Sympathy for The Devil.

I came home to find this book sitting by my front door the other day. It hadn't been posted from Amazon, as the address was torn off the envelope that it'd been sent in. The envelope had also been opened and the invoice removed. I thought that maybe it was a present from my mother, but sadly when I went into the back garden to feed my chickens I saw something that made my heart almost stop. The Devil. Now, The Devil is a chicken I used to own, it went insane and attacked me in my own home last year. The police ended up tazering it. The recovery from that attack took months and is by far the worst thing I have ever been through. You can imagine what it felt like to open my back door and come face to face with the limping, half-featherless bird that presented itself to me. Obviously I slammed the door and once I'd finished hiding under the kitchen table, I observed from the safety of the kitchen window that The Devil seemed different; he was limping, as I say, and cut a pretty pathetic figure of a chicken. He was just wandering about near the door of the coop.

I armoured myself in my baseball helmet, shin pads, and jumper with a pillow shoved up it. I also managed to get a couple of couch cushions up each leg of my trousers and, like the brave man that I am, I headed out onto the battlefield. (I also picked up my electric tennis racket that I used when I had the wasp problem.)

I needn't have bothered; The Devil wasn't limping, as I first thought, he was staggering. The patches where his feathers where missing looked burnt. It was like he'd only just been released from police custody after the attack on me last year. I was sure the police said he escaped, though. My paternal instinct kicked in as I could sense that he wasn't in a state to attack me; he had a playful nibble on my jumper, but it wasn't much. I wasn't stupid enough to take him back into the house, but I did lie him down in the hay and I got him some water and a bit of seed. By the end of the evening we were both shattered, so I covered him with a little towel, which he tried to eat, sat him up in the position sick chickens like to sit in, and left him to sleep. The next morning he was still alive and seemed a little more alert than before. I have a theory that he has been kept in secret chicken prison somewhere and tortured for information.

I'm still a little bit worried that once I've nursed him back to health, using this book as a guide, that he'll attack me again, but what can I do? Rolf Harris would be furious If I didn't help him. It's just not the Rolf way.

I've decided, based on the information in this book, that he was sexually frustrated when he attacked me. It seems his chicken genitals are deformed in some way, so being around all the hens in my coop must have been sending him crazy. It doesn't explain why he only attacked me and not the other chickens, but it's the only thing that makes sense. The book has great diagrams and I've learnt much about chickens. I even know which ones are girls and which ones are boys now, which is something I never knew before.

I'm in the process of building another coop, just for The Devil. I'll give him another chance to behave himself. If it doesn't work I'll see if I can get my cousin Jeff to do the trick that he keeps going on about where you pull off the chicken's head and they still run around. I don't believe it myself, but Jeff keeps offering to show me, so that might be the perfect chance. Also, as Jeff is staying with me now, there is another male in the house, so The Devil might even attack him next time. Then he won't be able to make jokes about how I was in hospital because of a chicken, because he will be too.

If you have chickens and you need to know more about them, then this is the book for you. Without doubt.

-Brian

ROSALLINI BRONZE TONE EMBOSSED FLOWER OLD STYLE WOODEN JEWELRY BOX CASE

Treasure chest.

I found this while out walking. I'm not sure what it's used for, but I know that the gamekeeper from the manor house wanted it back. He was furious that I wasn't a kid that would do exactly what he's told anymore. I remember Chopper from when we were kids trying to scrump apples from the manor's orchard. He was always well over the top. Most people would chase you down the road at the very most. Chopper would get on his quad bike and chase us all over the fields. We used to like it before he got the quad as he'd do it on his bike, and he had no chance of catching us on that. When the quad started showing its face, we had to jump in the river to get away. Bobby nearly drowned one time. Chopper didn't even try to help, either.

So it was with some satisfaction that I was able to tell him that no, I wasn't going to give him the jewellery box back.

Things got a little heated and he made all the threats that he used to, only this time I didn't care. He made a move to grab me. He obviously didn't know that I'd been doing weights ever since I spent a few weeks in a young person's jail last year. I was easily able to control the situation. He was trying to get up after I'd laid him down (again, controlled) but I didn't hit him or anything, didn't need to, but wouldn't have anyway. I'm not violent these days, the anger management in jail helped with that. Being a nice person, I offered my hand to him so he didn't have to speak to me from the ground. He was in a different mood now, no longer the scary man he'd been up until this point in my life. He spoke to me in a different tone that I wasn't used to from anyone. It was clear he really needed this jewellery box. He explained that he needed to sell it to his boss, the fat Lord of the manor. He wouldn't go into too many details but offered me three hundred quid. I instantly knew it was worth much more than that, so started the game of hard ball early. 'Six grand,' I offered. He didn't like that and offered me five hundred. 'Eight grand?' I asked, raising an eyebrow in a way that let him know it would be going up more each time he asked to lower it. He moaned for a while about not having eight grand but then offered me a deal; if I would hand over the jewellery box, he would show me how to make as much money as I ever needed and I wouldn't have to break the law in any way. I flatly refused this as I've been made offers like this in the children's home and will never be stupid enough to agree to something like that again.

Turns out he didn't mean that and he explained the scam he had going. He buys cheap tat and sells it to Monty as something a really old famous person owned. He said he'd introduce me and get me in on it.

So this jewellery box I found isn't old, as I first thought, but it's worth more to Chopper than the £19.00 it's listed at on here. In the end we agreed that since he'd told me the scam before I handed him back the jewellery box that I would sell this one and not give him any money from it and he would put up with it or get found out.

The money I made was immense. I've bought all the clothes I'll ever need. I tried to reason with the old bag that I've been fighting with but she won't listen. I'm going to stop making her life hard and hope she does the same. If she won't, I suppose I could always hire a hitman and get her taken out.

-Denny

MET SUPER BUDDY CHILDREN'S CYCLE HELMET

I should have bought an adult size.

I'm writing this review as a warning to others. I purchased one with the intent of becoming the world's finest BMX rider. I bought the largest child's size there was. I know I should have probably bought an adult size, but Janet says that if I'm as good at BMXing as I am at building models, I should probably not bother spending loads of money on equipment. I assume she meant that I'd get a sponsorship deal in no time and wasn't referring to the time I passed out face down in Super Glue after building a model house.

However, I digress. When I bought the helmet I noticed a picture of a young child who was being helped up by a man who was presumably his father; anyone else would have been weird and I'd hate to think it was a warning against men who pick children up after accidents.

Furthermore, I noticed that the young lad was smiling, like the fall hadn't hurt at all, which is what drew me to this helmet; I thought if I was going to get a hat, then I might as well go for the one that hurt the least if/when it was needed.

Sex offender/father or not, the picture is wrong.

Last weekend I took my BMX up to the local Co-op where they have some steps at the back of the car park that lead off into the park. I was going to practice my rail slides, There were a couple of idiots messing about on the stairs. One of them had a towel wrapped round his head, pretending he couldn't see, God knows why, so I just did what the professionals do and had a protein break — baked beans, cold — and waited until they'd finished. They were clearly not as committed as me because they were gone within a couple of minutes. I'd already done a few jumps and grinds on the bench in the park, so was confident that I'd be able to manage the same on an incline.

It all went well. I pulled off the first one fairly well, only catching little Frank and his two pet bulldogs lightly on the crossbar. It was cold so the bulldogs had headed inside for the evening; had they not have, it might have been stomach ache time.

After a break and a can of Red Bull, which I purchased from the Co-op, I decided the best thing to do was have a bit of a run up. I reckoned the speed would give me a chance to pull off the rail in a jump and look great at the same time. So that's exactly what I did. I rode all the way to the top of the hill leading down to the car park; I figured I would brake if it got too much.

Wrong: my brakes didn't work. I noticed the wire had been cut. Still, being one of life's triers I kept my head down and carried on; reaching the steps, I lifted the bike into the air a little before I would have done at a slower speed, obviously. It couldn't have gone more perfectly. If there'd been a crowd there they would have definitely been on their feet and chanting 'We love Brian'. It really was that good. However, when I landed, and Lord only knows where it came from, a javelin entered my front wheel and caused me to go literally arse over bulldog and land on my head.

The helmet broke the fall somewhat, however, and this is the reason I'm writing this warning. I didn't have a smile on my face like the young lad in the picture; in fact, if it hadn't been for the imaginary crowd, I would have been in tears. My head hurt like merry hell and did for some days. I was sent home from work the next day as Mr Hogsbottom, my boss, thought I was drunk. The doctor had to write him a letter explaining that I was concussed; if he hadn't, I think I'd have lost the job my cousin, Jeff, got me.

I think it would be a good idea to change the picture on the front.

-Brian

SOFTLEAVES A100 SILICONE BREAST FORM

Not really what I needed.

Losing my nipples in a moped accident was never something I set out in life to make happen. It did, though, and it hurt. I've struggled with my self-esteem ever since. The patches of pain that remain where my nipples used to be have healed a little and have stopped feeling like a burning hot version of jogger's nipple. However, having no nipples is not what is meant for men, however pointless they may be and however much I used to enjoy pouring a little of the church candle wax on them, neither of which meant I didn't want them anymore. I did. I think we *need* them.

It's taken a while and hours of drunken Googling to come across something that might help my predicament. Well, I thought they would. These fake nipples looked like just that in the picture, I know as I've since been back and checked and I double-checked again before writing this review. Unfortunately, these are not fake nipples, they're fake breasts and not what I was looking for.

No problem, I thought, and got to work with my Stanley knife to get the nipples off, which I did with ease. The problem started when I pondered how I would fix the newly removed nipples in place.

Glue? No. Sellotape? No. Bra? No. In the end I went for a combination of string and Blu-Tack. It didn't really work, though, it just looked like I was wearing a bra, and I'm definitely not into that sort of thing, not like half the clergy I used to go to vicar school with.

I've decided that I need to accept that I just have no nipples. If I drink enough then at least I won't remember not having them until I try and pour the church candle wax on there again; I'll be in God's house then, though, so I'll be OK. He'll nurse me through the bitter disappointment.

I'm sure these would work for someone who either wants to appear as a woman or for an actual woman who has minimum knockers.

I hope they work better for you than they did for me.

-Father Frederick

FLYMO GARDEN VAC 2700

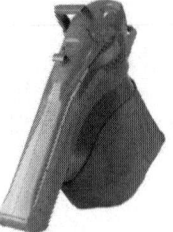

It sucks.

I knew I should have double-locked my chicken coop. I've had a problem chicken for a while, he ran away for a year but returned recently. I thought the electric shock treatment he'd been given by the police when he attacked me to within an inch of my life might have put him off dreams of escape. It didn't though, I suppose some chickens are just free spirits.

I'm not sure what exactly happened, but I do know that when I got home, my shed was gone and The Devil's distinctive black feathers were all over the garden. I got straight on the Internet to try and discover what happened. Most people suggested I asked my neighbour, but she wasn't interested in talking to me and just stuck her middle finger up at me through the pane of frosted glass in her front door. So I had to go back onto the Internet and delve further. It was only when Jeff got home and told me about birds that exploded when they ate certain types of things that we realised that is what must have happened. I do keep diet Coke and mints in my shed. I like to have a mint when I'm in the garden and I think mints make Coke taste so much better than it normally does. I must have left them out and The Devil had eaten them and exploded. He always used to break out of the coop before, too. I must have nursed him back to health so well that he was able to get out again.

This garden vac was a must, you wouldn't believe how many feathers one single chicken can spread around your garden. They were everywhere. Guts, beak and feet too.

I will suggest that you keep the vac on a lower setting as I also managed to suck up all my wife Janet's flowers, a couple of chicken eggs, a chicken leg, my own shoe and some of my cousin Jeff's hair, although the last one was on purpose and he got it back so he really had no need to moan on about it for the rest of the weekend.

I'm hoping I never need to use the vac for clearing exploded chicken's feathers again, but it did also work a treat for cleaning up all the plates that Janet smashed in the garden when she saw the state of her geraniums.

In closing, I'll say that if you want to save your house vacuum cleaner from breaking when in the garden, then it's a good idea to invest in one of these. I will, however, sound a note of caution. These are called garden vacs for that very reason, they are to be used in the garden. In the house they are WAY too loud and they will enrage your cousin, who could be trying comb his hair back to normal, or your wife who is angry at losing her garden to a gung-ho attitude with the vac in the garden. I thought they were moaning over nothing. At least they didn't have to worry about walking on exploded chicken in the garden. Cleaning a little bit of chicken guts from the kitchen floor when the vac emptied itself should have been the last of Janet's worries.

Never mind. I have a super clean garden to sleep in until I've been forgiven.

-Brian

SMALL SILVER WORKTOP BIN

A good place to store rotting food.

I've tried and tried to let go of the fact that Denny, the village anus, ruined all my veg; he was seen pouring something over them. I've never done anything to him, except steal all his clothes, and that doesn't warrant such a crime to be committed against an old woman.

    I'm sure there's something in the Bible about an eye for an eye so I decided the best thing to do was to cost him as much money as the shopping trolley cost and ruin his carpet. I saved up all the leftovers of my husband's dinners; however much it pained me to see some of my roadkill pie go to waste, I knew how much a bowl full of rotten food would stink a flat out. So, after two weeks, I waited until I saw him leave his flat in the morning then tipped all the food I'd saved in this tub through the letter box. To make sure that it was ground into the carpet, I chucked some large letterbox-sized rocks through, too. Although I had to stop after five as the smell was making me sick. If I'm sick too much I black out, so once my own dinner was running down the front door I made my escape, hoping that Denny would also tread in the leftovers when he walked in through the door.

    He didn't come back for hours and when he did, he didn't even notice the sick on his door. I watched as he put his key in the lock and tried to open it; one of the rocks had jammed behind it, though, and without thinking he just forced the door harder. It gave way a bit, but then bounced back as he was just putting his foot down. I was momentarily disappointed as the door pushed him back out; I needn't have been, though, as within a couple of seconds and after pushing and being pushed back, Denny was down, lying in a mixture of my sick and the leftovers. I almost cheered. It was better than a winning goal at Wembley. Covered, he was. If I'd owned a camera I would have taken a picture and added to the customer images section, but I've only got a webcam for when I go on Chat Roulette to scare the American college kids, and that is attached the computer.

This box, though, that is a good buy. It didn't stink my house out and I wasn't sick until I'd been around the smell for a while at the letterbox. It's airtight so you don't need to worry about having to keep emptying the food from it each day, which would kind of negate the point of having it. So I'm pleased to say that it works and should you use it for rotten food, like I did; you will have no concerns.

-Ethel

HOW TO BUY YOUR FIRST HOME (AND HOW TO SELL IT TOO) [PAPERBACK]

I'm going to need this.

I've been living in a village for almost a year now. I can't say I've completely hated it — the countryside is nice — but everyone is mental. Even my cousin. I thought that liking two bands so much you couldn't listen to one without listening to the other at the same time was mad, but Brian and his crazy ideas are even worse. There's kids running riot here and a fat old Lord that prances about the village looking down his nose at everyone. It's just a very strange place.

I've managed to sort out the bullying problem that my cousin was having, so it's time to leave now. I need a bus route near my house. They only come once a day here and I've been knocked off an electric scooter; it's just not safe.

So I'm buying my own house. And this bald guy looks just the kind of person who has no real friends, so has spent his life looking at broken houses. Probably talking to them, too.

I did email to go on one of his TV shows, but they've never replied to any of the three hundred and sixteen emails and letters I've sent, so I figured I'd have to read this book instead.

Well, it's that or move back in with Mother and I can't do that while her and Mr Hogsbottom are doing sex together. It's too weird.

Moving out is the only way. This book seems to have all the tips that the TV show has (for free) so it should be a great help.

-Jeff

INSIDE REHAB: THE SURPRISING TRUTH ABOUT ADDICTION TREATMENT — AND HOW TO GET HELP THAT WORKS [HARDCOVER]

Think it works!

I think we've finally managed to get my husband into a place where he accepts that he needs to go away and sort himself out. He can't do it while at home. He's not given a sermon to the flock for months. I don't even think he remembers that he is a vicar and he certainly doesn't know what day of the week it is.

We had an intervention. Me, Bishop Desmond, young Bobby and Bert, the farmer from next door, who was close to either calling the police or murdering Frederick due to his strange and drunken behaviour, things that Bert said I should never need to know about. I agree; I don't wish to know.

We had to plan the intervention well, and there were suggestions on how to do it in this book. We had to catch Frederick in the morning before he'd drank too much. This required that I and Bishop Desmond went round the house and removed all the bottles that Frederick thinks are well-hidden. In reality, they were just lying on tables or in drawers, it wasn't hidden at all. I'd just chosen not to throw them out, as he'd only waste more money we haven't got on buying more. This book explained that I'm as ill as Frederick is, although I think the authors should keep thoughts like that to themselves. That was the only comment in the book that I didn't like.

We kept a couple of light beers out, to stop the shakes and also to motivate Frederick to come into the room we were all in.

I can't say it was comfortable, but just like the book suggested, we put his chair in the middle of a circle of all our chairs, Desmond facilitated the group and then we all just laid into Frederick verbally and told him how his drinking had affected us. Bert forgot that I shouldn't hear about what Frederick had been doing with the animals and let rip. I didn't know it was him that put all the mousetraps in the field that Frederick had fallen into last year, but now I know it was, and it was because he'd killed Bert's favourite sheep. Frederick kept falling off the chair, so we plonked him on a sofa in the corner in the end. Bert offered to make sure he stayed awake by slapping him. He even started licking the palm of his hand in readiness for the slapping, but we all agreed it wasn't called for, much to Bert's disappointment.

Bobby didn't have much to say, he just sat there looking sad. I think that was what did it for Frederick, it was all too much and he screamed out that he needed help.

Once the others had gone, me and Bishop Desmond sat down with Frederick and went through all the different types of rehab. We've decided on a 12 step one as they incorporate God and Frederick quite likes God.

He's going at the end of the week. Desmond has found some money in the church roof fund to pay for it.

I'm looking forward to the break. I've told Frederick that if it doesn't work, then he's going to come home to an empty house as I'll be leaving. I mean it, too. I didn't say it just because it suggested to in this book; I will go.

If you need to get your head around rehabs then this is a

good book. I just hope you have the same result I did.

-Mary Woodford

BINATONE IDECT X5 SINGLE DIGITAL CORDLESS TELEPHONE

Great, but you need a BT line.

Now I'm earning a nice amount of money I thought I'd treat myself. Well, that and the last time I used the phone box someone locked me in there and I put my back out trying to get out. I'm fairly sure I know who it was: Chopper, the gamekeeper that I've been blackmailing. I won't be scared off by him and I have some ideas on how to get him back. But it can wait, I am earning money now and that is my new hobby. Revenge on Chopper, old Ethel the local mad lady, or Bobby my former friend turned church boy can all wait.

    This phone is great, it saves all the numbers you need, you don't need to leave your house and it's all cordless. The ring tones are good, I've picked 'Summer Breeze'. It'll let you set an alarm for if you need waking up, it'll take messages, and most of all it'll tell you who it is that's calling you, just like a mobi

    I've not actually used it for a call yet as I've got to wait for BT to come round and fix up the line. But when I do, it'll be great to walk around the house speaking to someone. At the moment I do walk round the house with it and it feels good, but I reckon it'll feel even better when someone is on the other end.

    I'll probably get into crank calling, too. But before all that,

PETE SORTWELL

I've got some money to start stacking from my new job selling cheap tat to Lord Monty as antiques.

It's been a great year!

-Denny

KARAOKE GF829 PORTABLE DVD/CDG/MP3G/CD KARAOKE MACHINE+ 535 TRACKS + 2 MICROPHONE +7"COLOUR SCREEN

Just what I needed.

I've always been into music. I've been in bands, toured with the big guys and even been on the radio, more than once. The band I tried to start in the village, that I decided I would retire in, didn't really work out. I only had one guy on a piano and the local idiot turn up to rehearsals. I was gutted. It took Emma, the landlady, at least three weeks to pull me out of my depression and it only lifted when she said she was going to do a karaoke evening. I couldn't wait. I made sure the man that was coming to run it brought with him all the rock god songs that make me look good. It was so exciting.

I wasn't going to let anyone with a piano or any idiots ruin it. So you can imagine my disappointment (and anger) when Brian the idiot walked through the door with his cousin, acting all hard. He knows I don't like him in my local. Yet he still came in wearing his girl's shirt and a girlier haircut. I couldn't let him wailing ruin it for me or anyone else, so I went over and told him to leave.

It all kicked off then. I won't bore you with the details as

I'm not an ego maniac. But the long and short of it is, I went too far and I'm now banned from the pub, so I've bought this machine to sing on while I'm at home waiting for the three month ban to finish. It's a great machine and the speaker is sufficient for the bass on the rockier songs.

If you like singing and music and you're banned from the pub until you sing a song with an idiot (the landlady's rules of me being allowed back in: three month ban or sing with Brian — I'm not doing it), this is the machine for you.

-Jock

GOOD BISHOP, THE: THE LIFE OF WALTER F. SULLIVAN [PAPERBACK]

An inspiration — hopefully.

What a year I've had. I look after all the vicars in the Southamptonshire area, and a very good job I do of it, too. I've never had to sack anyone. I've moved a few of the more 'touchier' vicars off to pastures new, but I've never had the need to sack anyone and I pride myself on that.

In a particular village, which I won't name, we've had to see the poor old vicar off to rehab. I doubt he'll be back in post, either. I've got someone I want to inspire into training to be a vicar and I think this book could be the very thing that completely makes up his mind to join the church, never have sex and to spend the rest of his days in the village he grew up in with nothing but old, mad people for company. What a life we offer here in the church!

Young Bobby has lacked purpose in his life, just like the great Walter. I'm sure reading about how much action a man like Walter took in this short, short life, will make his mind up fully.

Well, that and the huge rectory that I can offer him for nothing should he take up a career in the church. It's all there for Bobby to play for, I just need to make sure I 'motivate' him enough so that he makes the right decision, for all of us.

God bless you all!

-Bishop Desmond

ABOUT THE AUTHOR

Pete is 33 and lives with his wife, Lucie; daughter, Lilly; and their pet sofa, Jeff. He's been writing for just under three years and they've been pretty eventful; well, more eventful than he thought sitting on Jeff, typing, would be, anyway.

First published in the *Radgepacket* anthology with a story he'd written during month five of his new hobby, Pete's now featured in a total of ten different anthologies and has been amongst some very fine company. (Although he was the best in all of them, he knows that because both his mum and Jeff told him and they're both honest-to-God Christians ... possibly.)

Author of comedy e-books *The Village Idiot Reviews*, *The Office Idiot Reviews*, *The Idiot Government Reviews* and *More Village Idiot Reviews*, Pete has seen these books sell more than he ever thought they would, and he's hooked. *Dating in the Dark* is Pete's first self-published novel. His traditionally published novel, *So Low, So High*, was published by Caffeine Nights in June 2013.

Contact Pete:

Facebook:
https://www.facebook.com/pages/Pete-Sortwell/255907757862913

Twitter: @petesortwell

email: petesortwell@googlemail.com

OTHER TITLES

SO LOW, SO HIGH

Most people generally don't drink white cider for breakfast, don't use the aisle of Tesco as a toilet and don't steal from their family and friends. Simon Brewster does though. He's a doomed man. Living life day to day, stealing Edam balls and legs of lamb, ducking and diving his way from petty theft to dealer and back again. If he doesn't change his ways, he'll never see middle age, let alone old age.

He's seen his parents on their knees, crying, begging him to stop; he's been arrested by his former best mate; he's been hospitalised, all as a result of drugs and alcohol. It's just not enough to make him stop.

Simon lies to everyone, including himself. The truth is, he has no more idea why he does the things he does than you do. What he needs is a way out. But if such a thing exists, Simon hasn't had much luck finding it. He's powerless and his life is unmanageable to the point of insanity.

This is the story of Simon Brewster's last year using class A drugs. Join him as he crashes his way through police cells, courtrooms and display cabinets. One way or another, Simon will stop using drugs. But can the people that love him help him overcome his addictions before his addictions destroy him?

Available from Caffeine Nights Publishing.

THE VILLAGE IDIOT REVIEWS

Join Brian as he tries to woo the girl that works in the local shop; will passing out face down in super glue while trying to make her a gift hinder his chances of getting her to go out with him?

Will Father Frederick, an alcoholic vicar who has a slight issue with stalking, be able to win back the heart of a woman he loved a long time ago?

And will Ethel, who thinks that throwing hard rice instead of confetti in a bridegroom's face is an acceptable form of sport, be able to catch one of these two losers in love with her trick as they step out of the church on the happy day?

Written entirely in the form of product reviews, we guarantee you've never read a book quite like this before. Hilarious and wholly original, *The Village Idiot Reviews* pokes gentle fun at the more obscure corners of your favourite e-commerce sites – and introduces the most bonkers set of countryside dwellers since The Vicar of Dibley.

THE OFFICE IDIOT REVIEWS

There are all sorts of idiots we have to work with every day. Every office has them. Fortunately for most of us idiots in the work place are few and far between. However, Hogsbottom Plugs, 'the home of bath plugs' has a higher concentration than other workplaces, from the MD down to the cleaner, they're all Idiots.

Read the trials and tribulations of this idiotic workforce as they explain their recent life events through reviews of things they've bought. There's Donald, who try as hard as he does, simply cannot get the office junior to notice him, let alone drink some of his special, sleeping tablet-laced tea. Learn how Jeff gets his own back on the people who mock him by re-enacting a video he saw on YouTube involving seagulls, and watch in horror as the over-worked cleaner tries to solve the mystery of who is making his job of cleaning the toilets worse than a job cleaning toilets is already.

If you've ever worked in an office, then this is the book for you. You'll recognise the office sex pest, the liar and the moaning admin worker who's been there longer than the chairs. Written in the form of product reviews, *The Office Idiot Reviews* is the second in the series of 'Idiot Review' books from Pete Sortwell.

THE IDIOT GOVERNMENT REVIEWS

We've all seen the news over the last few years, watching in wonder and disbelief at the situations the people entrusted to run the country get themselves into and then proceed to lie their way out of. Just imagine, and this won't be hard, that they were so stupid that they wrote reviews of the items that got them into or out of their latest bit of trouble and posted them online.

Ted Williebond is angry, not only at having to settle for running the opposition, but also for the bullying he had to endure at school by Cameron Davies and Gary Osburn, who now run the Government and don't mind pointing that out to Ted every time they see him. Join Ted as he foolishly leaves reviews of such items as Silly String, vodka and thick curtains as he tries his hardest to bring down the coalition.

On the other side of the fence we've got Daniel Dangly, a foolhardy old school politician from Southamptonshire who, try as he might, cannot outrun the press, who seem to stalk him for easy stories; and Elouise Munch, a career girl more concerned about who's defaced her designer handbag than the people in her constituency.

Running the show though isn't Cameron Davies or Ted Williebond; in fact it is Betty Rivers, the CEO of Information Inc.

It can't work out well, can it?

Welcome to *The Idiot Government Reviews*.

THE COMPLETE IDIOT REVIEWS

The first three 'Idiot' reviews books are now available from Amazon in e-book format as a handy box set.

DATING IN THE DARK
Sometimes Love Just Pretends To Be Blind

Jason is single and has been for all of his 32 years. It's depressing. But not as depressing as being told by his mother that he looks like Humpty Dumpty — after the accident. With a face that not even his own mother can love, it's hardly surprising that he'll try anything to get a woman to go out with him, even if it's only for a single date. With little interest in anything other than his quest for a woman and a nice bit of cod and chips, Jason needs to think outside the box if he's going to find someone who'll give him a chance. Along with Barry — his best mate — Jason comes up with the only thing he thinks will work: dating a blind woman. However, to do that, he needs to pretend he's blind himself, which is a lot harder than you might think ... especially when guide dogs are so hard to come by. Eventually Jason's efforts pay off and he meets Emma, a pretty professional with a host of friends. When he takes her out, they instantly hit it off. But will Jason be able to fool both Emma and her best friend Jerry into thinking he's blind? With everything to play for, Jason faces the biggest challenge of his life, and nobody — especially not him — can see how it'll all turn out.

Printed in Germany
by Amazon Distribution
GmbH, Leipzig